PRAISE FOR *EASIER*

"Chris' ability to share insights and wisdom with humor, depth, and simplicity makes this book a direct hit. Every chapter is full of relatable and transformative takeaways for business, leadership, and life. *Easier* leaves an impression, creates powerful internal shifts, and stays with you long after you read it."

—Barb Patterson, Transformational Coach

"A master coach at the top of his game, Chris Westfall has an uncanny knack for striking at your core. A deceptively simple message delivered in an approachable conversational format, *Easier* will have you reframing your perspective on life and wondering how you can get more out of it, with less."

—Aaron Powell,
Founder and CEO Bunch Bikes, *Shark Tank* Season 12

"Chris Westfall provides a brilliant blueprint for personal transformation from the inside out."

—Karen Mangia,
Vice President of Customer and Market Insights at Salesforce;
author of *Working from Home* and *Success from Anywhere*

"The unexpected format and captivating story pulls deeply on familiar emotions and experiences through its rich detail, characters, and exquisite storytelling. However, *Easier* is more than just a well-told story. It challenges the way you think about your life and career, offering a wealth of insight on maximizing the potential of both."

—Christopher Lind, Founder and Principal Advisor, LearningSharks;
former Chief Learning Officer, GE Healthcare

"Who doesn't want to make things easier? In this book Chris shares 60 strategies to activate peak performance. You'll certainly find multiple ways to unlock yourself inside of these coaching conversations!"

—**Alisa Cohn,** Executive Coach and author of *From Start-Up to Grown-Up;* #1 Startup Coach in the World at the Thinkers50 Marshall Goldsmith Coaching Awards

"Chris Westfall drops anvils of truth from the highest perches and lets them crush the reader's cemented perceptions of identity."

—**Ken Orman,** Recovering Mortgage Banker; Writer/Producer of *Freeing Josie* and *From a Distance Dad*

"What a wonderful book, filled with stories, lessons and humor that would inspire anyone to find an easier way to live life. There is always a better way and Chris certainly helps the reader find it!"

—**Flip Flippen,** New York Times best-selling author of *The Flip Side,* founder and CEO of the Flippen Group

"Chris' masterful storytelling, imagery, and character development read like a great novel. From the first paragraph the story kept me emotionally engaged, reflecting on my own experience and ego, and somehow made me freer to absorb the underlying wisdom and lessons with little effort. A truly great read!"

—**Mark Bowles,** 8-time venture-backed founder, inventor, venture investor, and award-winning TV producer

"Chris' book is a realistic example of how to break free from routine, misery, and frustration - and come out with a clear realization for the next chapter of your life."

—**Jeffrey Hayzlett,** primetime TV & podcast host, speaker, author and part-time cowboy easier

CHRIS WESTFALL

easier

60 Ways to
Make Your Work Life
Work for YOU

WILEY

Library of Congress Cataloging-in-Publication Data

Names: Westfall, Chris, author. | John Wiley & Sons, publisher.
Title: Easier : 60 ways to make your work life work for you / Chris Westfall.
Description: Hoboken, New Jersey : Wiley, [2022] | Includes index.
Identifiers: LCCN 2021044591 (print) | LCCN 2021044592 (ebook) | ISBN 9781119834571 (cloth) | ISBN 9781119834618 (adobe pdf) | ISBN 9781119834595 (epub)
Subjects: LCSH: Employees—Coaching of. | Executive coaching. | Personal coaching.
Classification: LCC HF5549.5.C53 W47 2022 (print) | LCC HF5549.5.C53 (ebook) | DDC 658.3/124—dc23
LC record available at https://lccn.loc.gov/2021044591
LC ebook record available at https://lccn.loc.gov/2021044592

COVER DESIGN: PAUL MCCARTHY

SKY10030306_110521

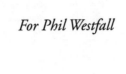

For Phil Westfall

What do we live for

if not to make life less difficult

for one another?

GEORGE ELIOT
AUTHOR OF 'SILAS MARNER' AND 'MIDDLEMARCH'

CONTENTS

PROLOGUE

You know what frustration feels like.

Unmet expectations. Regrettable observations. Unfortunate confrontations.

Maybe you don't believe you deserve more. Lots of people feel that way.

Most people feel frustrated and they just call it "life" and they ease on down the road. Even if that road is a dead-end street.

Once upon a time, there was a man who wanted a change. A change from frustration and freedom from expectations. He decided to try a new highway, to see where it might lead.

He was successful. And also not. He had achieved a lot. And also not. He was diligent. And also not.

He wanted more. He wanted a change. He was frustrated and he didn't want to wait for his life to change.

He thought that no one needs coaching.

But he saw that the people who really want to win never go into a game without it.

He wanted to play the game at a new level.

Maybe even change the rules.

Or find a new team? He wasn't sure.

He met a guy – a Coach – who said he helped people turn frustration into fascination. Said he transformed lives and had the track record to prove it. Launching businesses, changing careers, changing lives. The invitation wasn't a sales pitch.

The frustrated man was curious. He agreed to a conversation with the Coach.

Here's what happened next.

CHAPTER 1.
THE ARRIVAL

"I need you to be lazy," the Coach said.

Driving through the neighborhoods of manicured lawns, the Client had peered only at the road right in front of him. His attitude, regarding the interior of the car, the nearby traffic, or the amount of gas in his tank, was not lazy. He was not glancing at the palm trees that bordered the lawns. He did not take shortcuts. He did not wander off of his chosen path in a lazy manner. The four-hour drive had made his imagination work harder than the engine, leaving him wondering if he would find any real answers in the conversation ahead. The leather on the driver's seat was comfortable, but he was not. Because he was never, ever lazy.

Intent on his destination, he turned. But only when the GPS said so. He knew, deep down, that the navigation would reroute if he made a wrong move. But he didn't want to risk it.

On the drive, the Client was preoccupied with two objectives: getting somewhere and leaving the past behind. The first half of his plan was going well. Gripping the wheel tightly, he found himself on a broad residential boulevard. He had reached the Coach's street.

He still managed to drive past the address. He was lost in thought. Recalculating, he got there.

"Welcome," the Coach had said, and opened the front door. The Client and Coach exchanged greetings and walked through the house. They passed through two French doors and entered a large outdoor patio.

The Coach sat cross-legged on the Client's right. Underneath the ceiling fans, the two men had planted themselves at a right angle to each other, on overstuffed neutral-colored chairs. These were the kind of outdoor seats where you could spend an hour or two and not notice the time passing.

Beyond the open doors on the patio, the lush green backyard gave way to some slight rolling hills in the distance. Three brightly colored noodles bobbed against the side of the pool. A large rock formation, sort of like an elaborate four-foot-high kitchen backsplash, snaked around part of the backyard. The rock formation provided a small waterfall for the pool. Elegant tin roofs from neighboring houses floated above tightly trimmed hedges. Further to the south, the gray shadow of office buildings and construction cranes punctuated the landscape. Austin's skyline sat on the horizon like fingers on a hand.

The Client had been "coached" before. Mostly accountability stuff and goal-setting junk that lived somewhere between grit, willpower, and getting over yourself. The corporate coaching felt like having another manager in his life, with weekly meetings designed to help him to be all that he could be. He wasn't sure if it was a punishment or opportunity. Often it felt like both. He didn't want to sign up for that ride again.

Lazy seemed like a terrible idea.

He already saw himself as a mistake that needed to be corrected. A plan that failed because he failed to plan. Even when things went right, he could have and should have done more. He had risen in his career by being hard on himself. That pressure gave him an edge, kept him sharp, made him want more than the next guy. Nobody had ever told him to be lazy.

The suggestion was a loud fart in an elevator. He didn't appreciate the context, the source, or the repercussions. He looked down at the sweat clinging to the outside of his iced tea glass. His lips tightened and his teeth clenched. He looked at the Coach.

Back at headquarters, the Client's division was in the toilet. He had separated himself from the office by over 200 miles, but he carried blame and regret with him everywhere he went. He anguished over every detail, haunted by negative results. His business development job focused on acquisitions and growth. But the company hadn't even invested in any interesting technology in the last two years. He was, in his mind, completely ineffective.

He wanted control. Control and confidence. So he could do what needed to be done. He wanted out of the death spiral that had gripped his organization. He wanted freedom. Options. A new perspective. Not a lazy one.

He was here to make a change. Find a fresh start. The numbers weren't working. But, by God, he was. Even now, far from his office, he was still unable to leave work behind.

The division was tanking. He wanted to quit his job. He needed answers.

Lazy wasn't one of them.

He needed to fix a broken situation. He didn't need to sit here trying to fix a broken man.

He stared at the condensation on the glass of tea. He was going to resign in the next few months, if he could get this Coach to help him to find the courage to do so.

He didn't know he would be fired in five days.

Coaching was a fool's errand, he reasoned. Not today, not with this guy, not with me. No way.

Another error needed to be corrected.

Lazy? No, thank you.

The Client stood up. "I've made a mistake," he said. "I'm . . . I'm not doing this right now."

The Client turned, stepped around the chairs, and walked back into the house. The front door opened and closed. The Client was gone.

CHAPTER 2.
THE REALIZATION

There is a way to do it better.

Find it.

THOMAS EDISON
INVENTOR

Twenty-six seconds later, there was a quick double-knock on the front door, and it swung open. "Sorry, I forgot my cell phone," the Client half-shouted, as he reentered the house. The Coach was standing three feet away from the swinging door. He was holding the cell phone in his outstretched hand.

The Coach wore tan jeans and leather boots, a charcoal T-shirt, and a black watch with some heft to it. He was smiling, emphasizing the lines around his eyes. Grinning, actually. The Client took back his phone and began to apologize.

"I'm sorry," he said. What he said next spun out of him like a fork in a garbage disposal.

"I'm sorry I left like that; I just have a lot of obligations and a lot of things that I need to do – lots of stuff on my mind that's really pulling me out of our work and this conversation. Even though when I made the appointment it seemed like a good idea, I am not really in a place where I can focus on myself right now, because I just . . . well. . . . Uh, I can't seem to . . . yeah. What it really *is* is just something that, uh, half the time I don't even know myself, but I just feel like I can't really be here right now. I hope you understand and again I am really sorry. I also have to say that I don't understand where the hell you were going with that 'lazy' remark and I'm just not in a headspace where I can really unpack that, so I think it's best if I just leave."

The Coach chose his next words carefully. "There's no need to apologize. You have to do what's right for you. I support that. I'm here to support you. Whatever shape that takes is A-OK with me. I get it. Deadlines. Details. Obligations. I've been there myself, more than once. But before you go, why don't we just drink one glass of tea? One glass. Let's relax together, for a minute. And if you don't like the tea, or the conversation, then we can reschedule or whatever we need to do. No obligations. No pressure. It's just a conversation, right?

"And you never have to apologize," the Coach continued, hoping that those words landed. He was sharing more than just a courtesy. "Ever. Here, there are no mistakes. Only choices. And whatever they are, I respect your choices. You wanna sit back down?" he asked. "The tea is pretty good."

The men walked back out to the patio. They sat in silence.

The Client noticed a row of Italian cypress trees, standing like 40-foot-tall soldiers, waiting for battle. Perched in the blue sky, white cirrus clouds floated above the pointed green trees like a bunch of lazy hippies. Lucky bastards.

He turned to the Coach. "Nothing is easy for me," he said, apropos of nothing and yet somehow covering everything.

He continued, "Hard work is all I've known. If I'm lazy, how can I move forward in my life and in my career and . . . and . . . well, how is being lazy going to help?"

"People think of lazy as an activity, like eating potato chips and watching Netflix. That's 'lazy,'" the Coach said, uncrossing his legs. "And you're right – as an activity, 'lazy' is a horrible place if you want to get anything done. Other than binge-watching a show or growing your waistline, being lazy seems like a strategy for getting nothing done. We all know that being lazy is the opposite of being productive!"

Deep insight, the Client thought to himself.

"But as an attitude, lazy is actually brilliant. Consider your experience of being lazy on a lazy Sunday afternoon. Have you ever experienced a lazy Sunday afternoon?"

He had. The Client loved lazy Sunday afternoons. He began to share some memories of time apart from obligations, work worries, and schedules. He easily recalled times when he could do whatever he wanted; it was a rare treasure. Play with his kids, work on a project around the house that really mattered – the Client had several stories to share of time spent by himself, with his family, just exploring the outdoors sometimes. He confessed that he even enjoyed potato chips and the occasional Netflix binge, which made both men laugh.

"Me too! But wasn't that what made lazy Sunday afternoons so fantastic?" the Coach said, agreeing with him. "You got to do exactly what you wanted to do? You never wasted time doing something you didn't want, unless you wanted to waste time, and then the time-wasting thing just kind of turned from a label into life."

The Client chimed in, "And I lived it, and loved it, and all was well with the world." Were both men smiling?

"But you still had work on Monday, right?" the Coach interjected into the Sunday memory excursion. "Why didn't you spend your Sunday worrying about the week ahead?"

"Because that's not how a lazy Sunday works," the Client told him straightaway. "You stay in Sunday, you stay with the activity (or lack of it) and just enjoy the moment. Why would I think about the week ahead when I'm enjoying a lazy Sunday?"

"That's the kind of 'lazy' I'm talking about," the Coach said. "You don't waste time or energy on a lazy Sunday. Even if it looks like you're wasting time, you're actually not really wasting anything; you're just going through a kind of unconscious discovery of whatever it is you want to do next. Am I right?"

The Client took a healthy sip of his iced tea. He realized he hadn't had anything to drink since Waco. The Coach was telling the truth: this was good tea. He drained half the glass.

"Let's talk about being lazy in a new way – in a way that's super-kind to yourself," the Coach continued. "When you want to do something, what if you did it with a complete economy of action? Where you took only the actions that would maximize your results? Because, if you have a lazy attitude, you will always find the way to put in the least amount of effort to get the maximum impact."

The Client was interested in impact. He knew all about putting in effort. Hard work was the key to creating results, a fact that had been drilled into his head by well-intentioned teachers, family members, and that coach-manager person he had met with a few years back. Life was meant to be difficult. Even when it wasn't, it still was. That was the way he was wired. Or so he thought.

Until today.

"Lazy as an action plan means doing nothing. But lazy as an attitude is more like a lazy Sunday afternoon," the Coach explained. "On a lazy Sunday afternoon, you're not going to do anything that you don't want to do. And if you choose to do something, like working on your car, painting a room, hiking with your kids, or just making a spectacular sandwich – whatever it is that you like to do – you're not going to waste any extra energy. You're 'actively lazy.'" He leaned in for emphasis. "Actively lazy means that you are keenly invested in what you are doing and making sure that you're not wasting your time or your energy on anything that doesn't make you really happy. Unless, of course, you want to waste some time on something. Which is still part of the attitude – your state of mind – a lazy Sunday afternoon. There's nothing you can do that is a mistake, on a lazy Sunday afternoon. Because you are not on some artificial schedule, if you're really enjoying your day.

"Here look at this," the Coach said, handing the Client a small 3x5-inch card that was hidden underneath a black leather portfolio on the nearby coffee table. The Client read the printed words out loud, a quote from Bill Gates.

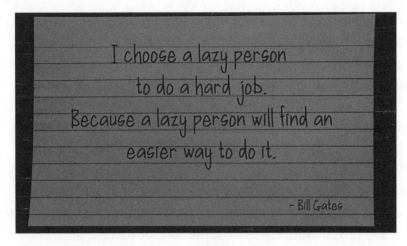

I choose a lazy person
to do a hard job.
Because a lazy person will find an
easier way to do it.

– Bill Gates

The Client sat back in his chair, as deep and as far as he could. The Coach took a sip of iced tea. He looked out at the trees to make sure they were still growing. Made sure no new buildings had been added to the distant skyline. Counted the clouds.

"So, that's it?" the Client asked. "Just be lazy, or actively lazy, and everything gets easier?"

The Coach looked out at the great outdoors. "Does it look like life has some kind of shortcut that you just haven't figured out yet?" He smiled as he spoke. There was kindness in his voice, even as the Client knew he was being teased. There was no malice or judgment. Both men knew there were no shortcuts. "I'll tell you a secret," the Coach said, leaning toward the Client and putting his hand up to emphasize the whisper. "Anything can be made easier. Anything. Maybe not easy, but easier.

"You've already discovered the choice that's easiest: walking away. Doing nothing. Embracing the status quo and giving it a big fat kiss," he said, laughing. "But easiest isn't necessarily effective, is it? I mean, if we bail out on the conversation, or the opportunity, or the relationship, how can we ever know where it will go? Not exploring is the easiest thing. But how will that help you – or anyone – to grow? To see things in a new way? I mean, discovery: that's what we're here to do, right? Regrets and missed opportunities aren't easier. Ever."

He leaned back in his chair. "Some things can never be made 'easy.' Fixing a rocket while it's flying through space, for example: not easy. Performing a liver transplant: not easy. Working in a business where competition is fierce, customers are fickle, and technology doesn't always cooperate: not easy."

"So basically, every business?" the Client interjected. He was starting to remember why he came to visit this guy.

"And every relationship." The Coach chuckled. "But we can go about our understanding and our business, our relationships and basically every aspect of our lives in a way that's easier. Easier is where life's better, where we find freedom. Clarity. Confidence. It's where we don't struggle and suffer and wish and try to manage the whole entire world. We can perform and produce and connect and just live, in a way that's easier."

"What if everything could be easier," the Client said, neither a statement nor a question.

"What if life could feel like a lazy Sunday afternoon?" the Coach added. "Not because you tell yourself some lie and decide to hallucinate while you're awake, but because you understand where things can actually get easier. And if you're wondering what things I'm talking about, I mean everything."

"I know this much is true," the Coach continued, shifting in the overstuffed patio chair. "I know exactly how many ways there are to make things easier. And so do you."

A bold statement, the Client thought to himself.

The Coach looked over at him. "You know exactly how many ways there are to make anything easier. Easier, in every aspect of your life."

"Everything you said makes sense except the part where I already know how many ways there are to make things easier," the Client admitted. "Because I don't."

"Well, the answer is the same as the number of ways to win a game," the Coach said. "A game of football, tennis, Parcheesi . . . you name it. The answer is also the same as the number of ways to paint a painting." The Coach took another sip of tea. He waited.

"The number of ways to win . . . ?" The Client's mind flashed on a soccer game – football for the Manchester United fans in his life – while trying to figure out how a painter would create a painting. "Games are complex. Seems like a painting is really a matter of choice or interpretation," he said after a moment.

"And not all paintings – or painters – are created equal," the Coach returned, adding "or equally."

In the Client's mind, it seemed like there was only one way to win – the way that worked. And the way to paint a painting? The one way that made sense to the artist, he guessed. Surely there was more than one way to paint a painting. He had tried his hand at painting once. Flashing back to soccer games, 90 minutes on the pitch left lots of room for choices and options and corner kicks and yellow cards and he was not going to *Ted Lasso* this, so how the hell could he figure it out, really?

"I . . . I don't know," I said.

"You're exactly right," the Coach said. "Because we can never know all of the ways to win in a game. Or all the ways to paint a painting. Because the number of ways to win, the number of ways to create a masterpiece, and the number of ways to make things easier is always infinite."

The Coach refilled both glasses from the silver pitcher on the side table nearest him.

Infinite? And unknown? Even with a refill, the Client was still thirsty.

"Our conversation centers on the unknown. A part of that exploration is bringing what you already know into clear view. Here's what I've seen, working with thousands of clients: if I say something, but you don't see it, it doesn't exist. Right? Even if you think I've achieved 'enchanted guru' status in your eyes – which I hope you don't, but whatever – you're always going to fall back into your own viewpoint to evaluate everything I share. As well you must; we all see things through our own eyes."

"I'm going to share things with you that come from my own experience, my education, my understanding of science and business and all kinds of things. But whose experience will you trust the most? The answer is always your own."

"So don't believe anything that I say," the Coach said flatly. "Trust nothing. Evaluate everything. Walk out if it sucks and feel good about it. You already know how to go with your gut. If what we're doing doesn't serve you, let's find what does. Remember: you are always the Client.

"Service is here," he said, swiveling his head with hands outstretched to take in the entire patio. "A service designed to take care of you. You have someone in your corner, right now," he waved and smiled, like a child saying hi to the clowns at the circus. An oversized, toothy grin matched the overenthusiastic wave. The Client chuckled.

"Someone is here to help you on your journey, if you will allow it. With your permission, we will look in the direction of new possibilities. Not in the direction of my experience" the Coach said, "but your own."

Shifting to a more serious tone, he explained, "I'm glad you came back. I'm glad you're here."

The Coach saw something of himself in the Client. Which is to say that the Coach saw something of himself inside each of his clients. The two men were different in age, education, and life experience. Yet the Coach saw something that connected them. The Client wanted to figure things out. The Coach knew he wouldn't have to.

"Run our conversation through this three-word filter," he said, revealing another card that was on the coffee table, hidden underneath a legal notepad and some markers. The Coach pointed at the card for emphasis.

The three words were written in red:

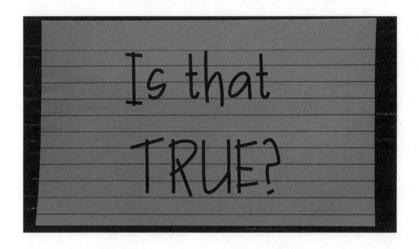

"We're going to look into the unknown, so we can see new possibilities. That's where possibilities live, right? Opportunities, too. Innovation and new ideas always come from the unknown. Just like all the ways to win, I'm not sure what you might see for yourself. My job is to point, to share, to question. To help you to play your game, your way. And to assist you to see what's been there all along. Like the South Pole."

"The South Pole?" the Client asked.

"Have you ever heard of Robert Falcon Scott?" the Coach replied. The Client shook his head.

"He was a British explorer. He led a team to discover the exact location of the South Pole. Unfortunately, a Norwegian dude by the name of Roald Amundsen beat him to it. The year was 1911, and that was when Amundsen discovered the South Pole.

"Except that's not true," the Coach said, pausing. "The South Pole was always there. Amundsen didn't discover it. He was just the first to reach it.

"Reach into your experience, as we continue our meetings," he added. "Not your past work experience, or your education, but the place where your experience – the way you relate to the people and circumstances around you – is coming from. That experience of a lazy Sunday afternoon, for example. That place could be a useful reminder of what's possible. After all, for some people, work feels like play – not the other way around. You know what I'm saying?"

"One thing that always exists, no matter what we say or what happens to you or where you go or who you meet: you always have a choice. And the choice is always up to you. You can choose to grind it out, relying on force of will and navigating your DISC profile[1] or whatever else looks like it makes sense. Or you can move in a way that's easier. And I hope you will. But the choice is really up to you. Always up to you," he said, nodding at the Client.

"We work together to reveal what can help you most. Because, when things are revealed, you act from a place of understanding, not expectation. From a place of insight, not just knowledge," he said. The Coach stood up, touched a hidden light switch on a support beam, and activated the ceiling fans above the two men. "And when you understand what's really available to you, everything gets easier."

"But that still doesn't always mean that I will do it, even when I see it," the Client confessed. "I can think of countless times in my experience that I saw a better way, and I didn't seize it."

Sitting back down, the Coach said, "I hear you. Me, too. But there's an easier way. In almost every aspect of life, things can always be easier. We both know it. There is a way to access new understanding and then to take action on it and that way is always and forevermore easier – if we allow it to be. Do you hear that?"

The Client nodded.

"How about . . . how about we look at fifty ways to make things easier? Do you think that would help? You decide what those things are – what topics matter to you. We'll find fifty ways to find ease and clarity and even 'active laziness' inside every aspect of your life. What do you say?"

"Fifty ways?" the Client asked. "How about sixty?"

If the number of ways to win really was infinite, the Client reasoned, then 60 different aspects of infinity would be an easy target to hit. He came to see that there could easily be 60 ways to paint a painting, not just one. He remembered that some artists had painted over their original artwork, and he shared that with the Coach. Some had probably thrown out the canvas entirely and started over – resetting an infinite capacity. And weren't colors infinite as well? Possibilities entered the conversation.

"Okay, sixty it is," the Coach said.

The Client asked, "Are you sure you have enough tea?"

"Could there be sixty ways to make my life easier?" the Client wondered to himself. Then, out loud, he asked,

"How would I know how to take action?" He was asking the Coach and the clouds and the patio furniture. "How can I get out of my own way?"

"The first step: be lazy. Decide that you are going to explore how life could be like a lazy Sunday afternoon. Start there," the Coach said.

The Client sat back in his chair, as the Coach added, "Now we have fifty-nine to go."

Note

1. *DISC* is a common personality profile assessment used in corporations and organizations. Developed in 1940 by Walter Clark, based on the work of William Moulton Marston from the late 1920s, the acronym DISC represents the four personality types: (D)ominant, (I)nfluence, (S)teadiness, and (C)onscientiousness. Profiles are a combination of these characteristics, providing insight into the dispositions and working styles of team members.

CHAPTER 3.
A COMMITMENT EMERGES

It's never too late to be

what you might have been

GEORGE ELIOT
ENGLISH NOVELIST AND TRANSLATOR
REAL NAME: MARY ANN EVANS

The Client wrote down the first of many new ideas:

WHAT MAKES THINGS EASIER?

1. *Live life like a lazy Sunday afternoon.*
2. *Easiest is "do nothing." But regrets and disappointment are never easier.*
3. *There's never just one way to win. Infinite possibilities = more choices = easier.*
4. *Discovery makes things easier. Look for the discovery.*

"What's the easiest commitment you can make?" the Coach asked. The Client was silent.

"As we begin this journey, it would be useful to understand *commitment*. Commitment is a huge part of results; you see that, right? But what may be equally powerful is understanding the nature of commitment. Because if we understand the nature of a thing, we understand how it works and how to use it. Right?"

The words resonated with the Client. His engineering background was going to serve him well here. He was ready to commit to something other than who he was, right now. He desperately wanted a change, even though he bailed out because he didn't think he could get there. He was settling into the conversation.

He didn't know what was waiting for him in five days.

"Have you heard of Imogen Cooper?" the Coach asked him. He had not. "She is one of the greatest concert pianists in the world. At the ripe old age of twelve, she decided she was unhappy and unsatisfied with the conservatory work she was doing. She wanted more than what her teachers could give. So her parents investigated opportunities in two places: Paris and Moscow."

"Where was she living at the time?" the Client wondered, recognizing that those two capitals were a long way from the capital of Texas.

"She was in North London. Her parents decided to enroll her in a French music school. The choice was regarded by many as a mistake: pulling her out of a traditional educational environment so that she could concentrate solely on the piano seemed . . . extreme. Cooper devoted herself for the next six years to becoming a concert pianist, seeing her family only on holidays, living and learning in Paris year-round. Was this kind of commitment too harsh, too much to ask? Some folks in the UK thought so. But no. Not for her. Not for Imogen Cooper.

"I'm sure the training was rigorous, the hours were long, the practice sessions intense. For someone else, it might have looked impossible. Leaving home before seventh grade, living in a foreign country, making the kinds of commitments necessary to become a virtuoso – can you imagine? But for Imogen Cooper, the commitment didn't look difficult, or arduous, or extraordinary. Do you know why?"

"Perhaps she was insane," the Client offered.

"Artistic brilliance can look like madness sometimes," the Coach said, chuckling, "unless that brilliance is part of your *identity*. What might seem like an impossible commitment to you or me was a much easier choice for her. Not without difficulties and challenges, but her choice was a commitment made easier by this one single factor."

The Client remembered learning to play piano as a kid. What could have made it easier? He wished he had known that back then, but sports and girls and other things captured his imagination more so than sharps and flats.

He reflected on the commitments he had to make in order to move into his current career, and his current position. He was no stranger to commitment: he'd been at his current company for ten years. His commitment – his career – was a huge part of his identity. He wanted that identity to change. He was here to discover how to make that change and make it easier.

The Client saw that the Coach was asking him to commit to himself. "A commitment is what is required to create any progress in your life. A commitment to your *identity*. Because nothing is easier than committing to be who you are."

The Client wrote down the words.

> 5. *Commit to who you are (IDENTITY) – nothing more, nothing less.*

The Client heard something inside the words. A commitment to himself. That felt like a lazy Sunday afternoon. Getting stuff done but doing things on your own terms and your own time. Because you always commit to yourself on a lazy Sunday afternoon.

Unfortunately, beyond his career, he wasn't sure he knew who he was. In five days, he would find out.

CHAPTER 4.
A DARING RESCUE

The past reminds us.

It does not define us.

ANONYMOUS

"I don't really know if I like myself," the Client said, frankly. The Coach had asked for radical honesty and had promised the same. "I don't know if I want to commit to the guy who overplans and underdelivers and finds fault with himself and others at every possible turn." He explained how his division was struggling amid massive market changes. Bids were lost. His team had survived a pandemic, but new products and new competitors were turning every effort into a struggle. His identity was tied to a losing battle, and he wanted out.

"I want to know how to commit to the self or my 'self' or some kind of 'self-life' where I see the self that I can believe in."

The Coach folded his hands in his lap.

The Client continued, "I had a corporate coach, when I was in management, and she used to tell me to believe in myself. I asked her which self I should believe in – the self that just ate a bag of Oreos, or the self that yelled at Josh in accounting (he deserved it), or the self that lost out on the promotion to a board member's nephew? 'Cause all of those 'selves' are right here and available, I told her. Right here on my 'self-shelf,' which I thought was kinda clever. She didn't. She shifted gears and started talking about my attitude. Said I had an appetite for confrontation and lack of coachability." The Client shook his head. "I thought I was just being honest."

"'Believe in yourself,' for me, is hard to believe," he continued. "I know people who are ragingly insecure, and yet they are very effective. Wealthy. Successful. Very good at their jobs. These people are caring parents, devoted partners, you name it, even though they question themselves at every turn. Really, that insecurity and self-doubt is my story, too. I had

a boss once who said that it was his insecurity that gave him
his edge. He always knew the other shoe was going to drop.
He used to say self-confidence was overrated." The Client paused.

"Sometimes I feel super-confident, and then a meeting
doesn't go my way. Then I feel self-conscious and somehow
things manage to work out okay. So how am I supposed to
know myself, when it's always changing? That identity thing . . .
I don't know that I have an identity that I can believe in. I'm not
sure it makes sense to try and make one up."

"I know what you mean," the Coach said. "I had a client
who came to me looking for executive presence and greater
ability to think on her feet. In meetings she found herself unable
to respond to questions quickly, and her boss had told her that
she needed to pick up the pace. 'I'm not able to provide quick
answers when people ask me point-blank questions, and put me
on the spot,' she told me."

"So what did you do?"

"I asked her a point-blank question and put her on the
spot," the Coach said. "I wondered if there was ever a time in
her life where she had to respond to something with split-second
accuracy, without even thinking about it? She told me that
there was.

"Without hesitation, she told me of a time when she was
snowboarding and blazing down this mountain when she went
over this mogul, revealing two young boys, maybe eleven or
twelve years old, standing in her path. The pine trees had
hemmed the boys into a pocket where escape was impossible.
What were they doing there? She had no idea. But one of them
was about to become a pancake. There was no way the kid on
the left was gonna move in time to be safe. The realization hit
that kid's face as the other boy yelled and screamed for him
to look out.

"She dug in on her snowboard, in a nanosecond, shifting to the right. She went up a small hill, changing her angle and launching herself up off the snow. She caught the boy in midair, wrapped him up like a burrito, and fell in between two of the pine trees. The two landed safely in a snowdrift, avoiding a nasty accident and probably saving that kid's life."

The men both considered the near disaster that turned into a rescue. The Client broke the silence.

"That's a big change from not being able to respond at work. Was she the office slowpoke . . . or the savior on the ski slopes?"

"Both," the Coach answered. "The woman stuck in the office meeting, unable to respond or reply, was the same woman who instantly saved that kid's life on that mountain. What changed? How was she able to be so responsive on the snow? Because that mountaintop answer might be the exact same reason she's often unable to respond to her bosses and peers at work."

Same person, different outcome, the Client thought to himself. What caused the dramatic shift? Necessity? Mind over mountain – or meeting?

The Client thought of times in his life when he had been stuck, unable to make a decision or a choice, and when he was able to effortlessly respond in the moment, just like the woman on the snowboard.

"What do you think," the Coach asked the Client, "was going through that snowboarder's mind when she was barreling down that snow-covered mountain and those kids showed up?"

The Client considered possible answers. Fear. Frustration. Another f-word, perhaps?

But then something new showed up.

"Nothing," the Client said. "She probably wasn't thinking of anything at all."

"What do you make of that?" the Coach asked.

"Well, we all have the ability to act out of instinct. To act without thinking," the Client said. "Which is typically the way that I describe my mistakes. Not some daring rescue on a mountain."

"Consider a field-goal kicker in a high-stakes football game," the Coach countered. "The team is behind by one point, only a few seconds are left on the clock. The field goal will put three points on the board. So the kicker is there to win the game. Become the hero. Or suffer the consequences of missing the big moment. Where does the kicker put his attention? On the fans in the stands? On the field goals he missed in practice last week? On what his coach told him last Tuesday? No. Thinking isn't the way to make the field goal. You've probably heard it a thousand times: *keep your eye on the ball.* Do what needs to be done – and playing back memories, or playing to the crowd, or listening to some story inside your head isn't going to help you to put that ball through the uprights.

"When we have more on our minds," the Coach explained, "we don't react quickly. Sometimes we can't react at all. But, underneath all our thinking, everyone has the ability to do what's needed. Not by acting thoughtlessly, but by seeing an important aspect of human nature. Because for me, and for my snowboarder client, for that field goal kicker, and probably for you as well, when we have more and more on our minds, we turn into morons."

The Client chuckled – not because it was hilarious, but because it was true.

"When we have less on our minds, we can access a new kind of lesson," the Coach said. "None of us is at our best when we are lost in thought. Underneath our concerns, considerations, and constructs, we all have the ability to do what's needed in the moment. If we can get out of our own way, we see it. We see the lesson, or the less-on, of greater capability."

"As I spoke with her," the Coach continued, "my snowboarder began to realize that she wasn't locked into a pattern of slow responses – it was a choice based on her thinking, not an unmovable aspect of her personality or hard-wired part of her DNA or anything like that. The reason she was being slow at work wasn't because of some failure in her intellect, or because she was trapped in some unbreakable pattern of behavior. No. Quite the opposite, in fact. She saw that, when she had less on her mind, she was more powerful and more capable than she realized. When she remembered that the woman on the mountain was the woman in the meeting, she saw new possibilities open up. She saw that she could respond more quickly, because she had done so before – and knew that she could do so again. I wonder if that's true for you as well?"

The Client knew what it was like to be lost in thought. He wasn't that different from the snowboarder sometimes. Still, he wasn't sure how he might respond in an unexpected crisis. In less than a week, he would find out.

CHAPTER 5.
A NEW IDENTITY

When life takes away,

something of greater value

is always given

in return.

MICHAEL J. FOX
ACTOR AND ADVOCATE

"Let's take a walk," the Coach said. The men went through the back patio doors, around the house, and exited through a large iron gate at the side of the Coach's house. Once they reached the sidewalk, the Coach wondered if the Client would consider identity in a new way.

"When we spoke, my snowboarding client and I, she began to see that her identity in the office looked really fixed and rigid. Like a mindset, you might say. But when she considered what happened on the slopes, she saw that who she was was not fixed. Her identity wasn't something rigid, where she always had to stumble and falter in high-pressure situations.

"She saw that in the office she was responding to being in a new job – like anyone would. She was hesitant to begin offering guidance or opinions too quickly. It wasn't a pattern of behavior or personality flaw or failure in her identity or anything like that. What she originally called an issue she came to see as some *wisdom*. She saw that taking her time wasn't an error but part of the necessary learning so that she could get comfortable with her new role. When she accessed some compassion and under-standing for herself, she began to realize that the woman on the snow and the woman in the office were the same person. She was able to 'zoom out' on the situation, instead of looking at her office responses under a microscope, then making the wrong diagnosis."

"How do you do that, exactly? Zoom out, I mean?" the Client asked.

"When the snowboarder was trying to 'figure out' why she was slow to reply or answer in certain situations, she was 'zooming in,'" the Coach explained. "On the mountain, she didn't 'figure out' how to save that kid, it just came to her. She recognized that insights come to us when we get out of our own way.

"When she stepped back at work, like an artist might step back from a canvas to take in the whole picture, she saw some new possibilities. Namely, that almost anyone would be hesitant and behave in the way she was behaving, if they were brand new to a job. *How* she was, in a particular situation, wasn't *who* she was.

"Her identity was more than what she realized," the Coach continued. Sprinklers showered the lawn on their right. A thin puddle was forming on the sidewalk in front of them. Just outside the range of the sprinkler system, an agave plant the size of a bathtub was resting in a rock garden. The corner of the yard was marked by desert plants and succulents, surrounded by white and tan gravel. The Client was silently amazed at how things were growing in this part of the world.

"What if your identity – who you were – wasn't on your mind at all?" the Coach asked.

The men came to a trail, bordered by a green iron gate that separated the neighborhood from nature. They turned right and began walking into a wooded area, leaving the sidewalks, streets, and shrubs behind.

"There's a misunderstanding around identity," the Coach was saying. "First, that it is fixed – like you noticed. You've seen introverts who have been the life of the party, for example, or extroverts who enjoy being alone. If you can see this fact with some compassion, you can see that we all have an identity crisis in some form. Namely, that our identity has taken form.

The form of thought." The men were walking into an open field; a stream flowed in the distance.

"What if identity was more like this stream?" the Coach said. "The stream is always the stream, but it's never fixed or rigid. Even when it's frozen, which doesn't really happen much in this part of the world, it's never completely without movement. Our thoughts flow constantly, like the stream, changing and shifting and meandering." He picked up a leaf from the trail, walked over to the stream, and dropped it in.

"We think identity is who we are. Right? We say things like 'That's just the way I am.' We identify with our jobs. Our neighborhoods. Our mistakes. My client said she was slow to respond, couldn't think on her feet. That was her identity. You know where it came from?"

The Client wasn't ready to dive in on this whole stream thing, "Her life and her choices informed her identity – that was where it came from."

The Coach smiled. "Identity for her – just like identity for you and me – came from her thinking. Her identity came from her interpretation of her life experiences."

"Her thinking?" the Client asked. "So, her imagination?"

"That's another word for thinking. Which is why it's such a slippery slope to try and believe in yourself, as you said. Because our thinking creates our identity and our thinking changes from moment to moment." The men stopped under the shade of some large oak trees. Nearby, an enormous growth of red and orange bird-of-paradise flowers exploded out of the surrounding greenery. "What if your identity wasn't something to consider, or manage? What would that look like – and what might change?" the Coach inquired.

"In the boardroom, the snowboarder was lost in thought. 'What if I don't have the right answers? What if I say something

I can't walk back later – would they fire me? Is Linda looking at me, and what will she think if I say what I really feel about the new warehouse in Wisconsin?' You get the picture, right? We've all been there. Second-guessing ourselves. Making up problems that need to be solved. We all get lost in thought, trapped in an identity of our own creation. A creation that's based on a misunderstanding."

"Namely, that we are important?" the Client guessed, not really believing the words but trying to find where this identity crisis was going. "Where does the stream fit in?"

"We have to handle this stuff gently," the Coach said. He turned to the Client.

"When it comes to who we are, it's easy to be really hard on ourselves. *Of course, if being hard on yourself were going to work, it would have worked by now.*" The Client nodded his head. He took a deep breath.

"What happens when you're not thinking about yourself? When you're not wondering who you are and how you are doing?" the Coach asked. The Client took a moment to really consider the question. "What is your identity, before you think of yourself?

"Look at that stream right there. Does the stream need to be fixed, or improved in some way? How about that enormous oak tree right over my head, the one that is giving me this perfect shade right now. Is that tree anything less than perfect? It's easy for us to see the perfection in nature, in a stream, a tree, or a flock of birds," he said, pointing up at a flock of birds as they passed overhead. "But we don't see ourselves in nature. We don't see our human nature. We don't zoom out to see the bigger picture. Because we are, quite literally, lost in thought. Thinking that we are our careers and our cars and our cares and everything else that looks like our identity. The truth is, when it comes to our identity, we just made it up. Who are you," the Coach asked him again, "when *you* aren't on your mind?"

The Client looked to his left. Then his right. His eyes glanced above and below, as he considered the question. "I'm just a guy, standing near this stream, out here in nature, talking to you," he said. "When I'm not on my mind, I'm just . . . I guess I'm just part of the world. Just a guy in the universe."

"Isn't that true," the Coach said. "Part of a universe that turns acorns into oak trees, and makes streams flow. That same universal presence somehow brings me these words and ideas to share with you. Seems like this universe is a kind place, when we allow it to be." The Coach tilted his head to the left, to see if the Client was picking up what he was laying down.

"Sometimes we have new realizations, and new ideas. Sometimes the universe brings disease. Pandemics. Disappointment. Loss," he said, looking down at the trail. The Coach took a moment to remember someone he loved once, someone who wasn't here anymore. He had stood beside him, under this exact same tree, once upon a time.

"In spite of my past, or because of it, I'm still here," the Coach said, bringing himself out of the memory.

"I'm still standing. Still moving, like that stream. My identity isn't fixed," he said simply, "and it doesn't need to be. Because my identity – like your identity, and the true identity of everyone on this planet – is part of something larger than myself."

"See, if we are part of something larger than ourselves, part of a universe that has our backs, a lot of things get easier. In contrast, if everything is up to me, I'll never be done with my work. But it's not up to me." He tugged on the sleeve of his T-shirt. "I have no idea where this shirt was made, or who made it. I don't even remember where I bought it. But, here I am, not running around like Tarzan on this trail because somebody, somewhere, made this shirt." He laughed to himself.

"Hey, here's an idea. What if nothing is up to me? What changes if I see that there are forces at work that have created this stream, and these trees, and this conversation – and those forces don't have anything to do with me, or with you?"

The Client noticed how the trees leaned over the stream, protecting it and providing shade for whatever creatures lived along its banks. The native grasses were punctuated with wisteria, sage, and wildflowers. On both sides of the water, the most beautiful blooms in all of Texas provided a banquet for the butterflies to consider. The stream was cradled in a green blanket, decorated with blooms of orange, purple, and red. Winged visitors floated silently about the flowers, resting on the calm winds. Amidst the stillness, there was motion. Motion inside the stream, inside the plants, inside the men. The Client considered how the trees and the stream always have enough. He considered the scene in front of him, and the absolute perfection of nature. The Client took a few steps, kneeled down, and felt the cool water of the stream.

"What if the Universe has your back," the Coach said, with a smile. "What if it's not all up to us? We don't have to make that stream right there flow. It's doing it all on its own, just like the plants that are growing and the birds that are flying, and whatever ideas might be buzzing around in our heads," he said.

The Client looked at his left sleeve. He was wearing a shirt from nowhere as well. He didn't know who made his shoes, or how the synchronicities of life had brought him to this moment. He was an educated man, familiar with science and engineering, but this conversation was pointing him toward everything that he didn't know. Where – or what – was an identity that made sense?

CHAPTER 6.
A BOLD PLAN

God provides the wind.

But man must raise

the sails.

ST. AUGUSTINE

"Look, I've gotta be honest with you," the Client said. "I'm here because I want some answers about how to leave my job. I want to start my own business. I've done it before but that was over ten years ago and a lot has changed since then. I know you're an entrepreneur and you've started several businesses, plus I know you've got a reputation for helping entrepreneurs to launch businesses and stuff like that. So I'm looking to you for some answers and some guidance on how to pull out of this job and get going with my life." His hand covered his stomach as he spoke. "I appreciate this conversation about streams and identity, but I don't see how exploring the nature of the universe and where our thoughts are coming from and all that is really helping me play the game of life over here."

"I used to coach people on how to play that game," the Coach said. "The game of life. I'd share my guidance and my instincts and my advice and quite often it was one or two steps ahead of my clients, so I looked like I was smart. Until I wasn't. Until what made sense to me clearly didn't make sense to the client, because of their experience or education or insight or my delivery or God knows what. I thought to myself, what's wrong? Is it me? These strategies worked for Jeena, Joan, and Jim! Then I started to realize that I didn't want to coach people to my own level of expertise or try to turn my past experience into someone else's results.

"I mean, if I told you how I entered that stream, and waded through it to the other side, and you wanted to get to the other side, you would listen to me, right? And I would tell you how I entered the stream and where I stepped on the rocks and how I dodged a frog and where I saw the fish and then, voilà, I came out on that bank over there," he pointed as he spoke. "And you can too, if you just enter the stream right there!" he said, his voice rising, as he pointed at three rocks that might be a good foothold in the stream.

Not a bad place to start, the Client reasoned.

"Except it's not the same stream!" the Coach continued. "Thinking you can imitate someone else to find what's missing is . . . well, what's missing. It's useful to learn from others' examples and gain other perspectives. But the most important perspective – the one that creates real transformation – is your own. Think about it: you're not me. Your stride is different, the weather is different, you might get stung by a bee, or slip on that rock, and then what? I'm not saying that my guidance isn't useful, but you have to consider that your path – your stream – is yours to discover. Some pointers are useful, yep, but what's really powerful is figuring out how to cross the stream on your own. Knowing that you can enter the stream on your own terms is the kind of coaching that creates transformation, not just tactics. Because transformation doesn't come from somebody else's experience. It comes from one place, and one place only. Real and lasting change requires *insight*. And the insight that will help you cross that stream? It's the insight that you are capable and resourceful and supported in a way that makes everything easier." The Coach looked at the Client.

"Here, let me give you an inoculation," the Coach said, pretending to stab a needle into the Client's arm, and deliver an imaginary vaccine. "This is a single dose of *resourcefulness*; it reminds you that you can do stuff, you don't need a template to follow, and it enables you to figure stuff out. Actually, you can already figure stuff out, but this vaccine helps you remember that fact even when you forget it. Remember, you have received the resourcefulness vaccine. I can tell you that it really works. Even if you don't trust this vaccine, your ability to figure stuff out is one hundred percent effective."

"But this vaccine to get stuff done, it's imaginary," the Client said, "you just made that up."

"Ah," the Coach said, "but having someone else give you a pattern and a worksheet for your life – they didn't make that up? That looks real to you? Doing what some mentor did in 2017 will create the same results for you today? That's a real strategy? Really?" He shook his head. "You have to play the game, where you are, and how you are, with a new kind of playbook."

The men continued walking, following the stream, as the Coach explained, "I've done a few things in my career that some people might call extraordinary – probably because they happened to a guy like me," he said, laughing at himself. "I've found that when you coach the player, the game takes care of itself."

Underneath a long row of trees, the Coach launched into a story.

At an outdoor café in Silicon Valley, two coaches were sipping cappuccino when a man wandered up to their table. "Please help me," the man said. Speaking in fits and starts, he explained to the coaches that he had amnesia. He asked both men to take him on as a client, and they agreed.

The first coach submitted the man to a series of personality tests. His IQ was off the charts. The man was well-versed in technology, software, and science, although he was prone to wild romantic notions and futuristic visions that seemed like pages out of a science fiction novel. The man could be belligerent, impatient, and quick to anger – often for no reason that the coach could understand. He was suspicious of authority and traditional systems, prone to repetitive behaviors, probably on the autism spectrum. Immediately, the first coach began instruction on how to become successful by leveraging his exceptional IQ and scientific knowledge – helping him to play to his strengths, which did not include dealing with people. He explained how to stay out of the public eye and cater to his introversion. He proposed extensive coaching to work on his public speaking skills, which were almost nonexistent. The coach crafted a plan to help the man to access success tactics, based on the coach's extensive experience in the energy industry. With his guidance and expertise, the coach reasoned, the man could find a rewarding career in engineering, or perhaps software. The first coach had a deep familiarity with those industries and careers and had coached countless scientists during his career. So he knew his advice would work.

The second coach took a different tact.

He quickly began doing everything he could to remind the amnesia victim that he was Elon Musk.

"If you understand who you are, and what you are capable of," the Coach explained, "whatever game you want to play becomes easier. Diving into the details actually isn't easier, although it looks that way because you think you have to figure everything out. That approach is based on a misunderstanding. Instead of playing the game, you think that you *are* the game. 'How can I leave my job?' is a great question. But let me ask you: don't you know how to leave your job?"

The Coach expanded on the question. "I mean, haven't you written a resignation letter before? Haven't you received one, from one of your employees? Haven't you had the conversation in the past, where you told someone you were quitting? Come on. You know how this dance is done. You know how these mechanics work!" The Coach was shaking his head.

The Client was silent. Yes, he knew how to resign a position. Yes, he knew what he needed to do. But why was it still so hard? "You've got to wonder," the Coach said, "why you haven't done it yet."

"The 'how to' isn't the problem, even though that's what it looks like on the surface. It's the 'want to' that's the real issue. Do you want to explain your choice to your wife? Do you want to face the blowback from your team members? Will there be people who are let down by your decision? Are you ready to deal with the disappointment, losing the consistency of your schedule, your salary, and the comfort that comes from knowing what's next?"

"Even if what's next sucks and keeps me awake at night?" The Client was looking down, asking the rocks and the dirt. He looked at the wildflowers, searching for some of that universal kindness and insight that the Coach was talking about. The Client wandered back on the edge of the trail, trying to find his next thought.

"Yes," the Client continued, half-talking to himself as he walked, "Exactly. There's a want-to issue here, disguised as a how-to. There's just a lot of unknown repercussions and I'm not sure I can cope with the fallout or if I'm ready for that level of change."

The Coach nodded in agreement, acknowledging the Client's honesty. He listened as the Client shared more about what he imagined those unknowns might look like. Financial considerations. Worry over his ability to find something new. Anxiety about where new opportunity might come from.

His fears would prove to be well-founded. While he was working with the Coach to "pack his parachute," his company was planning on pushing him out the back of the plane.

"Isn't it true that we have infinite possibilities available to us at every moment?" the Coach said, pivoting on his left foot and walking backward. Two steps later, he reversed the maneuver, directing himself to walk like the rest of the humans on the planet. The Client considered the pivot, both literally and figuratively. He stopped. He turned to the Coach.

"I guess so," he said, still processing the construct of infinity. "Like the different 'self' images I shared with my other coach. I was being defensive at the time, but now I see that I can access creativity and innovation at any time, if I choose to do so. My shifting self was just a changing thought, I guess."

"That's how thought works," the Coach replied. "We are living in the feeling of our thinking. Do you see that?"

The trail ahead revealed a grove of oak trees. "One person looks at this grove of trees, and says, 'Wow! I can't wait to walk through and see what's inside!' Meanwhile, another person looks at the exact same trees and says, 'I'm not going that way; I want to watch TikTok videos and eat Cheetos.'"

That was random, thought the Client.

"The point is this: is that grove of trees something to be enjoyed, or avoided? Are those trees a good thing, or a bad thing?"

"Neither," the Client said. "It's just a bunch of trees!"

"Exactly," the Coach said. "But it is our thinking – the way we process the world around us, from the inside out, that gives meaning to everything and everyone around us. We are not wired to respond directly to the world; everything – and I mean everything – passes through the filter of our thinking. We experience life from the inside out. Our feelings are a reflection of our thinking, and we assign values to an impersonal universe. Those trees are neither good nor bad; they are just trees. But every human being on this planet can and does make up a story – an interpretation – of the world."

"But that interpretation is just thought," the Client observed. "And thoughts are . . . well, what exactly?"

The Coach replied, "Thoughts are just thoughts. When we overidentify with our thoughts, when our thoughts start to take solid form and create prison walls and steel bars and reasons to eat Cheetos, we might want to look at that. Not manage that. Not control that. But consider that our thoughts are just thoughts. They don't have solid form, even when we think they do.

"Consider the man, trapped inside a locked room, no bigger than a closet. He twists the knob, and it turns in his hand, and he pushes with all his might. He pushes and struggles, shoving his entire body at the door – leaving him a bruised prisoner with no hope of freedom. He begins to panic. He wonders how he will ever escape, how he will ever find the strength or the wherewithal to push the door open. His thoughts begin to race, his palms sweat, he begins to imagine what fate might befall him if he can't push that door open.

"It never occurs to him that the door might open to the inside," the Coach said.

"Like, he wasn't really trapped in the room at all?" the Client wondered. The guy in the room, the Client realized, was trapped in the feeling of his thinking. "If only he could change the way he was thinking!" the Client said, sharing a realization.

"Trying to control our thoughts is actually the last way to create real and lasting change," the Coach said. "What makes it easier to welcome new thoughts is a simple understanding. Namely, that new thoughts are always on the way. Haven't you been completely stressed out and overwhelmed by your own version of the immovable door, and then . . . somehow . . . a new thought shows up? Is that magic, or is that the way that insight works?

"I suspect that for our prisoner, when his thinking settled down, he pulled on the door and found the freedom that had eluded him. It's counterintuitive, but when his state of mind changed from absolute panic, he saw new possibilities. That process isn't something to be managed or controlled but *realized*. Understood? Because if we see how thought works, we see that we don't have to control our thinking, manage it, or overidentify with it. Sometimes, we feel panic and constriction and all kinds of things, because we are human. But when we recognize our higher nature – namely, that new thoughts are always on the way – things get easier."

The Client considered the grass beside the trail, spreading out in all directions around him. Thoughts were like the grass, he supposed – always growing, always showing up. He was unable to imagine how many blades of grass there might be, just in this small patch of nature in front of him.

The idea of infinite possibilities, in the world of thought, became something he experienced. The nature around him pointed him back to his own human nature – an identity that was something before his thinking. And, just like the grass beneath his shoes, he didn't have to manage those thoughts, or control them, or overidentify with them. He was moving through a stream of thought, but at the same time able to choose different directions and desires. He could wade across the stream, for example. Or go off the trail. Or sit down, right beside the bright orange flowers that dotted the field in front of him. He was more than just his thoughts, to be sure. His thinking wasn't something to be managed, just something to notice – like a blade of grass, or a tree.

The Coach had picked up a stick and was dragging it in the dirt as he walked. "In 2020, scientists in Canada identified that human beings have over six thousand thoughts per day.[1]

The National Science Foundation found that the average person has about twelve thousand to sixty thousand[2] thoughts per day."

"So, which is it? Six thousand or sixty thousand?" the Client wondered.

"I'll have to give it some more thought," said the Coach, crinkling the lines around his eyes. "The point is: our thoughts are constantly changing, like the wind."

The Client nodded as the Coach continued. "When I worked with my snowboarder client, she came to see something that might be useful. I call it the YAHOO strategy, and it always makes things easier."

"Yahoo, like the search engine?" the Client asked.

"No, it's an acronym," the Coach replied. "You Always Have Other Options."

"So many times, when we get stuck, we get wrapped around an identity of 'that's just how I am.' You know what I'm saying?" he asked. The Client did know, because that was just how he was.

"We lose sight of who we really are when it looks like who we are is fixed, unmovable, and limited. That identity doesn't empower us; it restricts us. Keeps us tied to the patterns and prisons of the past. What can we do to make things more fluid and less fixed? That's where things get easier."

There was a quiet truth inside the conversation. The Coach chose his next words carefully.

"I'm going to lay something on you," the Coach said, lowering his voice, "And you may or may not be able to hear it, but just consider what I'm about to say."

The Client was curious about the request for permission, but he was here to learn. He encouraged the Coach to go on.

He did. "You are part of the universal wisdom and stream of consciousness that's all around us. Wisdom isn't reserved just for billionaires, or astronauts, or leaders of industry. We all have incredible power inside all of us. The power to access this universal intelligence. It's where our thoughts come from. I'm talking about that unknown force that's turning acorns into oak trees, making waves hit the shore, you name it."

"It sounds like you're talking about God," the Client said simply.

"I'm saying we are not separate from God," the Coach replied, "although some of my clients call that connection to source, universal mind, or lots of other things."

He continued, "Can you identify with that?"

For the Client, a door opened to the inside of his imagination. He didn't need a leap of faith to see that he was part of the universe, that he was part of something much larger than himself. What if he didn't get lost in labels, or dogma, and just looked at the way things are? What if he saw the tiny miracles happening in every minute of every day, both inside of himself and all around him? As he walked, he looked at the stream, and the trees, and the bright blue sky, as if for the first time. Because he saw something new.

In the flowing water, a heron of some kind stabbed its beak into the stream, creating a serious problem for whatever prey would soon be in its stomach. The universe brought both miracles and challenges. Difficulty and delight. Sometimes the sun shines, sometimes there is rain; he knew that. And, while it was no resolution or simple answer, he saw that injustice, disease, and even pandemics were part of nature. So was loss. So was pain. But he also saw that there was a kindness built into the system, to allow us to somehow find our way through it all. Life wasn't always pleasant; life wasn't supposed to be. But the world didn't have to be difficult, even in the midst of difficult circumstances.

Looking at nature, he saw his own true nature. His human nature. And he realized that he was connected to a source that wasn't separate. A source that made things easier. Not easy. Because life wasn't always easy. But this source that was driving the stream, and bringing new thoughts to mind, without fail: he could call it God. Or universal mind. Or Bob. Labels didn't matter. Discovery of his true nature did. That true nature was connected to the divine. The unknown. The source of everything seen and unseen. That connection wasn't "out there" – it was inside of him. He discovered he didn't need a priest or a rabbi to access the way things are.

The Client stopped walking. He turned to look at the Coach.

"Holy shit," the Client said.

Notes

1. Murdock, Jason, "Humans Have More Than 6,000 Thoughts per Day, Psychologists Discover," *Newsweek*, July 15, 2020, www.newsweek.com/ humans-6000-thoughts-every-day-1517963
2. Antanaityte, Neringa, "Mind Matters: How to Effortlessly Have More Positive Thoughts." Tlex Institute, https://tlexinstitute.com/ how-to-effortlessly-have-more-positive-thoughts/

CHAPTER 7.
COMING BACK HOME

You can't stop the wave.

But you can learn

to surf.

The men walked in silence, leaving the stream for the sidewalks and street signs. As they neared the Coach's house, he picked up the conversation once again, this time with a personal confession.

"So many times, when I've gotten stuck, I've wrapped myself around an identity of 'that's just how I am.' I'm telling you, I lose sight of who I *really* am. I'm not saying I'm someone who is spectacular or brilliant, while I fall in love with the smell of my own aftershave." The Client chuckled at the thought.

The men walked on. "I'm talking about how human beings are wired – or *Livewired,* as the case may be."

The Coach was referencing a book by David Eagleman,[1] a neuroscientist at Stanford University. Nineteen steps later, the two men entered the Coach's house, encountering a large sitting room where books lined the walls. The Coach pulled *Livewired* off the shelf and handed it to the Client. "Take a look," he said, pointing.

The book was filled with stories of people who had experienced dramatic loss – loss of limbs, hearing, sight, and more. Yet these people had been able to rewire their brains, literally, so that the part of the brain used for seeing, hearing, or walking was transformed. Repurposed. Reinvented. Their identities – and their capabilities – changed dramatically. How?

The brains of blind patients rewired their sense of touch to activate the occipital cortex – the part of the brain assigned to sight – creating new pathways. Touch activated the part of the brain reserved for vision, a fascinating story of rewiring inside the human brain. However, as the Coach pointed out, while learning Braille requires some work, rewiring the brain required no effort whatsoever, because of the way the system is built – because of our human DNA.

"Take a look at this, on page seven," the Coach said, reading over the Client's shoulder, "There are twenty times more connections in a cubic millimeter of cortical tissue than there are human beings on the entire planet." The Client turned to look at him, stunned. Inside a cubic millimeter? The number might as well be infinite.

"Identity isn't really about creating some persona, and trying to believe in it, or shattering some past belief system that doesn't work to replace it with something else," the Coach said. "An easier identity is one that's truer. More scientific. More universal. More real."

"Sometimes that universe that has my back has stabbed me in the back," the Client said flatly.

"Sometimes it looks like that to me too," the Coach confessed. "But facing life's challenges – and dealing with our identity – gets easier when we understand how we are all made," the Coach said, simply. "Life happens, I get it. But also, so does resilience."

"We all have the ability to change and adapt, often much more quickly than we realize, because of something called *neuroplasticity*. Our minds are never fixed, which is why mind*set*," – he emphasized the second syllable – "like a fixed identity, is based on a misunderstanding. Trying to set your mind is like trying to harness the wind. That's not how the breeze really works. And neither do we."

The Client read a passage out loud from page 16:

> The thrill of life is not about who we are but about who we are in the process of becoming. . . .

He flipped two pages at random, and these words caught his eye:

> Whether intentionally or not, 'plasticity' suggests that the key idea is to mold something once and keep it that way forever: to shape the plastic toy and never change it again. But that's not what the brain does. It carries on remodeling itself throughout your life.

"Identity is not fixed," the Client said, making the realization his own. He lifted his head and turned to face the Coach.

"YAHOO," the Coach whispered.

"Identity is an invention," he continued, as the Client closed the book. "A creation of our own thoughts. Reinvention is always possible. That reinvention is not a matter of belief. My snowboarding client saw it: reinvention is a matter of understanding. And understanding who you are – like understanding how gravity works – is something that is useful, regardless of personality type, Meyers-Briggs profile, or even your current belief system. New to your job, or ready to leave it, there is a design that is built into the system. Seems to me that the design is kind, and compassionate, even when we aren't. Embracing the system – embracing the way things are – lets me know that I don't always have to be on my mind. Embracing the system allows me to see that it's not all up to me."

"In fact, just because a train of thought shows up, I don't have to ride that train. Are you with me? That realization will help you find new solutions in the boardroom, and new levels of ease in your life. Just because you think your identity is a certain fixed thing doesn't mean it's true. Your personality can change[2] – you have capabilities available, anytime, anywhere. It's not about belief, really. It's about understanding."

"Wait a minute, my personality can change?" The Client was curious.

"Absolutely. Personality is not fixed. Which is why we don't need to fix it. Because we are born with this amazing DNA – the kind of DNA that Eagleman explores in depth in *Livewired* – which has adaptability at its core, resilience inside of it, and nothing that needs to be fixed."

The words were a powerful challenge to the Client's belief system. His mind was not set? Nothing needed to be fixed? His state of mind was becoming calmer by the minute. He sat down on a large armless blue sofa, as the Coach continued.

"Believing in yourself is difficult. Not easier. Trying to fix what's not broken isn't easier. It's redundant. Unnecessary. Like chasing your tail or trying to replace a perfectly good light bulb.

"Easier is understanding who you are. You are wired to adapt. To innovate. To create. That's not just your birthright, or mine. Resilience is built into the system: the human system."

The Client thought his identity, like his personality, was "fixed." Immutable. Immovable. He came to realize that maybe he played a role in creating his identity. Strangely, he didn't judge himself for creating his identity. How could he judge himself harshly for being human?

He wondered if he was discovering how to zoom out. Perhaps he was making some progress. What happens if things that looked fixed started to get a little more fluid?

He found some of the compassion that the Coach told him was part of his identity. He felt like he was experiencing that universe that had his back – the same universe that was causing his thoughts to flow and his eyes to blink, and billions of other things that were happening right now without his input or involvement. He was starting to explore being easier on himself.

He had an insight: he didn't need to believe in himself, if he understood how the system worked. After all, the Coach explained, even if we don't believe in gravity, it still works. No matter what our personality type, income, or self-image, if we trip, we will fall down.

"Gravity is part of the universe, right?" the Coach said, zooming out once again. "That universe has your back. You are a part of that universe, too, my friend. And that's the identity that makes everything easier."

The Coach asked if he could share the details of a conversation he had with his own coach.

"Wait a minute – *you* have a coach?" the Client asked.

"Of course," the Coach replied. "How can you be a coach if you don't have a coach? If you don't experience the power inside of a coaching conversation on a regular basis, how can you share that impact with others? It's like teaching someone how to swim when you haven't been in the pool.

"I've seen the value of coaching in my own life, as well as in the lives of my clients. The universe has my back, and I don't have to go it alone, so I don't choose to. Sometimes I lose sight of the possibilities that are all around me. Sometimes I forget that I'm part of this universal force, and I get lost inside my own thoughts. I'm human just like everybody else!" the Coach said with a grin. There was a parity, and a generosity, inside his conversation. The Client found his own wisdom easier to access, when he realized that there were two travelers on the journey. Two seekers, seeing the world from different viewpoints, but both with experiences and expertise and wisdom to offer.

"Here's what I know," the Coach said, "I'm always better when I have someone else in my corner. Not someone dragging me through the pain of my past, or scolding me, or offering a new set of expectations, but someone who's helping me to create the future."

The Coach explained how, during a particularly rough period, he had a moment of severe self-doubt. "I was explaining my concerns to my coach. I had all these deadlines. I was feeling overwhelmed. What she told me next kind of blew my mind." The Coach was sitting in a nearby armchair, looking at the Client.

"My coach lives in Southern California, and she loves to surf. I'm wrapped up inside the details of my deadlines, right? And she's talking about the ocean." He shook his head at the memory. "So, she's explaining to me that surfers have a saying, and the saying is this: 'The wave always comes to you.'"

He paused.

"When you are out in the surf," the Coach said, "you really can't do anything to make the wave come to you. And it always does. That's true, a hundred percent of the time. The wave always comes to you. When it does, you can get on your board and ride it. Or not. But the wave always comes to you."

"I know exactly what you mean," the Client explained. He talked about how his wife was from Hawai'i. When they were dating, he went out to Honolulu with her and took a trip to the North Shore, where her cousins, aunts, and uncles lived. It was his first time on a surfboard. A lifetime of skateboarding, plus waterskiing at the lake when he was a kid, and he was able to hold his own on that first day. His wife's favorite uncle told him that he was "pretty good for a *haolie*." He later found out that, in its kindest interpretation, the word meant "someone from the mainland."

"The less glamorous part of surfing is that after you have ridden a wave, you have to turn around and paddle back out. Likely right into oncoming waves that are part of the same set of the wave you just rode!" the Client explained. "These are waves others are riding in that same moment but you're having to go against them to get back out! It's just how it works, part of the game of surfing. But the fitter you are, the easier that is. My uncle – he wasn't my uncle at the time but now I think of him as my uncle – he told me, 'The ocean is my gym,' and he meant it!"

The Coach loved hearing this story and encouraged the Client to go on.

"What about when the wave of life kicks your ass?" the Client wanted to know. "What happens when the ocean throws you off your board?"

The Coach nodded his head as he sat back in his armchair. "What did your uncle tell you, when the sea was rough, or there was weather, or something else that made the waves dangerous or undesirable?"

"Ah," the Client said, remembering. "'When in doubt, don't go out.'"

The Coach nodded. "I heard it a little differently, but the idea is the same. 'When in doubt, wait it out.' In my experience, when my thinking is choppy, and low, and I'm in a bad place, I wait it out. The wave that I need? It's out there. Maybe not in the middle of a thunderstorm, or a tidal wave. But the next wave is out there, and it will come to me. But getting knocked off your board, isn't that just part of surfing? Isn't that how that game works?"

"Wait it out," the Client repeated the words to himself. Wow, what could be easier than that, he wondered.

He reflected on his third day on Oahu, when he was learning to surf. A storm came in while he was on the board, watching for the next wave. Two uncles hollered at him, pointing to the shore, and he followed their lead. Together they paddled in toward the beach. Back inside the family home, the Client took some time to acquaint himself with poi. He tasted

some of the freshest pineapple he had ever eaten. He wondered
if the Coach had ever tried kalua pig. The Client explained how
the pork dish is prepared, similar to pulled pork but using a
traditional oven called an *imu* that infuses the meat with an
amazing smoky flavor. The Coach was fascinated.

The conversation was evidence of the Client's own insights
and wisdom, and the value of experience. The Coach's job wasn't
to inject some level of guru know-how into the Client's head.
He wanted to point the Client toward his own know-how, so
that he saw the wind, the waves, and the world in a new way.
A way that worked. A way that supported him. A way that
supported humanity. A way that was easier.

The Client had lived an amazing life and the Coach was
here for all of it.

Later that day, the Client explained, the surfers went back
out on their boards. The waves were even better than before.

Patience was important. And always available, even though
the Client often had trouble accessing it. But patience: patience
was the time between the waves, or "sets" – because the waves
always come in sets. In between the waves, you caught
your breath.

The space between was a good place to be. It felt like a lazy
Sunday afternoon.

The Client remembered a teacher, way back in elementary
school, who told him, "Patience is a virtue." As a nine-year-old,
that was a lot to take in. He had asked her, "What the heck is
a virtue?"

He was still impatient. He was still looking for answers.

The Client explained that sometimes he felt like he was
trying to kick and push and tread water and do everything he
could to manufacture and manage the waves inside his career.

"Me too," the Coach said. "I know what you mean. Sometimes I feel like I'm standing on the back of a sailboat, and instead of letting the wind take the sails, I take all the responsibility. You ever feel that way? I try to be responsible for moving the boat. So I find a good place on the back of the boat where I'm blowing as hard as I can," he said, spreading his feet wide. The Coach started improvising a scene from the *Three Little Pigs*, where he huffed and puffed but nothing important happened. The Client laughed.

"Sailboats and surfboards, right?" the Coach said. "But something is supporting all of it. All of us. Moving us forward. We don't have to manufacture the movement. Something is making the wind and the waves come to you. Wonder what would happen if we realized that there were things moving us forward, caring for us, propelling us, outside of the sea? Maybe we'd quit spending so much time working on the front wheel."

"The front wheel?" the Client asked.

"Yeah," the Coach said. "We concentrate so much on the front wheel, in our careers. Like riding a scooter. You know how that front wheel is where you find direction, right? Professionally, 'working on the front wheel' means taking leadership courses, or learning how to modify a Salesforce object, or getting trained on how to onboard a new employee. Useful skills, right? Steering – you gotta have it! But where does the real power come from?"

The Client contemplated the question from his seat on the sofa. He was going to say the engine, but then he started thinking about bicycles, where there was no engine. What then?

The Client was nothing if not thorough.

"The back wheel?" he said.

"The back wheel," the Coach agreed.

The Client realized that, in some ways, he had been obsessed with steering the scooter in his career. He remembered going to the hardware store with his father when he was a kid. He would sit on the riding lawn mowers, the littlest one first. He would steer one green mower ferociously, then another, while his dad shopped.

As a kid, he thought he was really good at steering. Of course, those lawnmowers never went anywhere.

Over the years things hadn't changed much, he realized.

Gaining momentum, that was the hard part. Finding the power to move forward was elusive.

Scooters, lawnmowers, professional advancement. He wanted acceleration. Movement. More variety. But he was coming to see that movement wasn't all up to him.

He wasn't sure if the universe had his back. But he decided (at the Coach's encouragement) to just sit with the idea that the wave always comes to you.

"I've been knocked off my board on more than one occasion," he said. He was curious how the Coach felt about that observation.

"Yep," the Coach acknowledged his viewpoint. "I'm no expert, but I think falling down is how you learn to surf," he said.

"Imagine if a baby, just learning to walk, was picked up every time it fell down. What if its momma took that baby's legs and worked them, saying, 'Here's how you walk, baby,' push, pull, push, pull?" He pantomimed something in midair that looked like milking a very tall cow. Or was that gesture supposed to be "walking a baby," four feet above the ground? The Client wasn't sure, but it looked ridiculous.

"If a baby is carried all the time, it never learns to walk. Because it never experiences balance. Never finds its own footing. Never finds out what walking means, from the inside out.

"We have to experience falling down, so that we can learn to walk. Your uncles could have told you the A-to-Z on what it's like to get knocked off your board. I suspect that they showed you how to fall and how to go into the waves, right? My Cali coach told me some stories about those moves – pretty cool stuff. But hearing stories about surfing isn't the same as being at the top of the wave."

The Client nodded as the Coach continued. "Life is a contact sport. You have to get out in it and experience it on your own terms. Did you learn to enjoy the waves?"

The Client chuckled and nodded. "Yes, I love to surf. Love it. Even when I get knocked off my board. Because getting knocked off was just part of the game, really. I always got back up and tried again."

His resolve would be tested in five days. A tsunami was headed for his career.

Notes

1. Eagleman, David, *Livewired: The Inside Story of the Ever-Changing Brain* (Vintage Books, 2021).
2. Vitelli, Romeo, "Can You Change Your Personality?" *Psychology Today*, September 7, 2015, https://www.psychologytoday.com/us/blog/media-spotlight/201509/can-you-change-your-personality; see also https://www.psychologytoday.com/intl/basics/personality-change

CHAPTER 8.
DISCOVERIES

Your thoughts are like the artist's brush.

They create a personal picture of the world you live in

SYDNEY BANKS
AUTHOR OF 'IN QUEST OF THE PEARL'

Sitting in the living room, which he realized was also a home library, the Client decided to write down what he had discovered so far. The Coach wanted to give him some space and said he would check back in a few. The Client was interested in another peek at *Livewired*. He sat down with the book, alone, on the sofa.

Inside Eagleman's book, the Client read about how scientists wanted to see how quickly our brains could begin rewiring and adapting to new inputs. The premise was simple, as he discovered on page 20: "Our DNA is not a blueprint, it is merely the first domino that kicks off the show."[1] The show, he came to realize, was our incessant and never-ending ability to adapt. That adaptation didn't come when we were thinking of ourselves. Adaptation wasn't a function of self-image, belief, or will. Resilience was part of our DNA.

He read about a researcher, Alvaro Pascual-Leone, who was curious about how quickly the brain could adjust to extreme circumstances. Together with his fellow researchers, Pascual-Leone blindfolded a group of study participants, inducing blindness. The scientists witnessed *neural reorganization,* the same thing that happens with the blind, when they learn to read via Braille. The subjects' brains were literally reorganizing, remodeling themselves to the change in circumstance.

The changes were identified on brain scans, within *less than one hour after blindfolding*. Over five days, the blindfolded test subjects had begun rewiring their occipital cortexes – the part of the brain designed for eyesight – and showed increased sensitivity to sounds and words. Touching objects activated the part of the brain reserved for eyesight, just as it did for truly blind subjects. When the blindfolds were removed, the sighted participants returned to normal brainwave patterns within a day. The transition – the new wiring – was natural and effortless. Resilience and adaptation are built into the human nervous system, so there is no struggle or effort in order to access plasticity. The adaptation was like a wave, the Client realized, coming to all of the subjects in the study.

The Client realized that a blindfold of his own had been removed.

He came to see that his identity was more flexible than he realized. Maybe even infinitely flexible. What would show up, what might he discover, if he considered an identity without making himself the center of the universe? An identity that connected to the universe around him, instead of isolating him inside of it? An identity that allowed for the possibility that this universal life force, this energy, this adaptability, was inside his very DNA?

Could that wave be coming to him? Or was it already here?

He could be supported by that kind of universe. It might be easier to step into that kind of universal identity, instead of having to drive, control, modify, and fix his own personal self-image – instead of having to stand on the back of the boat and blow, like some maritime Big Bad Wolf, trying to move his entire life forward.

What if he stepped into an identity where he saw that he had the ability to adapt, to innovate, to create new possibilities – not by effort, grit, or willpower, but by simply being human? By understanding who he really was, beyond the thought bubble or identity construct he was trying to shape, control, and maintain?

No one was asking him to commit to anything more than who he was: a human being with infinite possibilities built into the system. He wasn't trapped. He was empowered, by both science and spirit. In a previous conversation, the Coach had called it "both, and," meaning that he was the product of both the known and the unknown, both the spiritual and the practical, the personal and the universal.

He found freedom, and resilience, inside a new understanding.

If he invented himself, he could reinvent himself. Or not. He could just be, without being on his mind. He could be "both, and." Whoa, that felt easier!

Reinvention was more like acceptance, or knowing, instead of striving or stressing. There wasn't some heavy exploration of the past, involving regression therapy, "shadow work," or a deep dive into the teachings of Carl Jung. In fact, he didn't have to do anything, if he simply saw what was going on.

Reinvention, like identity, was exactly one thought away. And what, he wondered to himself, could be easier than a thought?

As he read the words of the scientist, Eagleman, he began to glimpse that the human system really did have his back. He saw new insights into resilience. The pages were filled with stories of everyday heroes, extraordinary people who had overcome a wide variety of adversities, unlike anything he had ever faced, and they were thriving. The truly extraordinary part was that their experiences were, on the most fundamental level, ordinary.

For the Client, seeing the extraordinary inside the ordinary was the point: that human beings are part of an intricately designed, compassionate, and amazing system. The human system. The system that was part of this universe, that the Coach said had his back. A system that adapted to impossible adversities, just as he had somehow managed to adapt and move on from the losses and disappointments of his life. True, he'd never lost a limb or gone blind. But, he realized, he was blind to the power inside of himself until today.

Resilience wasn't something to be achieved through effort or struggle. Resilience was intricately woven into the fabric of the human system. The system that was designed to make everything easier. But how could that be, he wondered? What about loss, tragedy, perhaps even a shift in identity?

That identity shift was what he wanted: an easier way to become who he was meant to be. He was a seeker, pursuing a path toward personal freedom, trapped in a frustrating job that robbed him of his passion and potential.

He longed for a world where he found the courage to leave the career that no longer served him. He wanted control. His Coach – the one who asked him to be lazy – told him that the wave always comes to him, and he knew it to be true from his own experience in the sea. Surfing was unpredictable. But it was the unknown that put the fun into any function. Could he trust in the uncertainty all around him, in the same way he had learned to trust the rollers on the north shore of Oahu?

He couldn't control the waves, although, in his career, he had spent a good portion of his life trying to do so. "If it's going to be, it's up to me," was a line he had heard many times before. What if it's *not* up to me, he wondered?

What if the wave really did come to him? What if something new was on its way? What would that feel like? Not passive, he decided. Not "just waiting for life to happen." No way. Actively lazy was a concept that started to take shape.

What if he started living his life like it was a wave, riding and zipping around because it was fun? He could still have deadlines, and fun, at the same time. The world of "both, and" was starting to take shape, and he liked that identity. Because he didn't have to do anything, other than commit to who he already was. And then play the game. Of surfing, or life, or whatever it was he was on about.

Could he move away from the career identity that was the source of his finances and his comfort, his support system for himself and his family? Perhaps, if he saw resilience and resourcefulness as real possibilities. Could he change from the identity that caused his stomach pain and sleeplessness? He wanted to. He didn't want to keep waiting for who he was meant to be.

He wrote down what he had observed, focusing on what made things easier.

He rewrote the first five concepts, copying them over from his previous notes, and reflected as he added the rest:

1. Live life like a lazy Sunday afternoon.
2. Easiest is "do nothing." But regrets and disappointment are never easier.
3. There's never just one way to win. Infinite possibilities = easier.
4. Discovery makes things easier. Look for the discovery.
5. Commit to who you are (IDENTITY) – nothing more, nothing less.
6. YAHOO = You Always Have Other Options. Always available, always easier.
7. Don't believe in yourself. Understand who you are. It's easier.
8. The less you have on your mind, the easier it is (it = anything).
9. Identity is made of thought. Who are you when you're not on your mind?
10. Your true identity is based on an infinite level of creativity and possibility.
11. You don't have to wonder, "Who am I?" and "How am I doing?" These questions don't

(continued)

(continued)

  make anything easier, except self-
  consciousness, insecurity, and doubt.

12. *You can react quickly, adapt fully, and rewire rapidly; it's built into the system. Nothing is easier than being who you are.*

13. *Our minds are never fixed – accessing new ideas is easier than we realize.*

14. *"That's just the way I am," isn't.*

15. *If being hard on yourself were going to work, it would have worked by now. Compassion always makes things easier.*

16. *Reinvention is exactly one thought away.*

17. *The universe has your back.*

18. *You don't have to go it alone.*

19. *The wave always comes to you.*

20. *Start anything and everything by being easier on yourself.*

He was excited by the list. Larger forces were at work, and he didn't have to take responsibility for everything.

Then his phone rang. He pulled it out of his pocket. The phone number of the CEO appeared on the screen.

On the other end of the line, a fuse was being lit. In less than a week, his career would explode.

Note

1. Eagleman, David, *Livewired: The Inside Story of the Ever-Changing Brain* (Vintage Books, 2021), p 20.

CHAPTER 9.
THE DEPARTURE

Life has many ways of testing
a person's will,

either by having nothing
happen at all

or by having everything
happen all at once.

PAOLO COEHLO
AUTHOR OF 'THE ALCHEMIST'

He wanted to stay. The phone call made it nearly impossible to do so.

The coaching conversation was enjoyable. Insightful. He felt a sense of purpose, somehow, in between the patio and the stream and the books and the cards and the Coach. There was an understanding of the way thought works, and the spiritual nature of life, which expanded his own resourcefulness in powerful new ways.

He was glad he stayed. Glad he found some headspace to just . . . listen. It wasn't a lazy Sunday afternoon, but for a Thursday it was pretty good. His first day with the Coach was coming to a close.

A new possibility was taking shape, and it was easy to commit to – effortless, in fact. He was tapping into an identity that wasn't manufactured or constructed as much as it was realized.

There was a generosity in the Coach's words. No sales, no motivation, no nonsense. The Client experienced something that didn't exist inside his office environment: namely, encouragement.

The Coach wasn't paying him compliments or blowing smoke. The Coach was telling him who he was. Telling him what he was capable of. Their conversation wasn't based on some specious and hopeful viewpoint. It was based on science. Experience. Nature. And wisdom.

As a result, the Client was connecting to new discovery, although he couldn't quite articulate it. It felt like the kind of enthusiasm he had on the first day of school, or the anticipation on the last, when he was a kid.

Before the phone rang, he felt lighter.

Before the phone rang, he felt newer.

Before the phone rang, he felt closer to possibility.

The screeching of the cell phone was like catching ice-cold vodka in the face, complete with crunching ice, shattered glass, and a cracking hard slap.

The nuanced and supportive world of insights was crushed with a call.

On the other end of the phone, his CEO was disappointed. Perplexed. Frustrated. The Client couldn't tell if she was mad at him or at the situation or at the last lost bid, but she was mad at something. The situation needed triage, and explanation. She shared more bad news.

Numbers were going the wrong way. Always, always the numbers. He understood. So did she. They connected.
He listened.

Updates were needed first thing Monday morning. Could he deliver? She needed to know: would he be ready with the reports?

The Client, forever the good soldier, responded to the call of duty. The immovable object needed another push up the hill.

His stomach tightened. The old familiar clench.

"I'll be there on Monday," he said, knowing that his weekend had just vanished. The conversation ended as abruptly as it had begun.

He sunk into the living room sofa, folding his hands over his stomach.

"How's it going?" the Coach said, reentering the living room.

CHAPTER 10.
THE LOST WEEKEND

At its best, life is

completely unpredictable.

CHRISTOPHER WALKEN
ACTOR

The Client was unable to speak for a moment. The Coach sat down in a nearby Eames chair.

"You okay?" was all he said.

A verbal avalanche cascaded out of the Client. The latest request was further evidence of massive mismanagement, built on an inconvenient truth: his division was out of sync with what the market wanted. Despite the company's best efforts, or half-hearted tries, more nimble competitors were providing responses that went unmatched. He explained to the Coach how he loved to win, but the company and its products were ill-positioned to do so.

The Coach listened.

He heard the disappointment. The frustration. The veiled rage.

The Client felt strangled, shackled, subverted. He had ideas, but those ideas had fallen on deaf ears. Because his ideas required investment, or transition, or transformation – things that, for whatever reason, the senior leadership would not embrace. Why? He didn't know.

The CEO's request for more information was another shoulda-coulda-woulda exercise. It coulda been handled in real time by the software systems the Client had proposed. They shoulda gotten closer to the customer, before a "cone of silence" descended on the bid process, then they woulda shaped the proposal to their capabilities. The bid was lost, in part, because of outdated technology, and a lack of investment in innovation. An investment that competitors had made, but his company had not.

His job, in part, was to outline the forsaken investment for evaluation. The request was a rehashing of a similar exercise he completed prior to the pandemic. The Client wondered aloud what they had missed in the original report. The findings would be similar, although, he admitted, not the same, because of other new entrants and changing regulations, part of the technical details of his industry. Like a similar recipe with substituted ingredients, the Client explained that he would be starting mostly from scratch.

He felt alone. Isolated in his intentions. He was the lone ranger, finding justifiable investments that the CEO would not endorse.

He had to return to Dallas in the morning, and cancelled their Friday coaching session. He needed the day tomorrow, after the nearly four-hour drive, to touch base with some of the team members involved in the failed bid. On Saturday, he was attending a wedding. The event was an all-day affair, so Saturday was spoken for. The report, he knew, would be written on Sunday.

His lazy Sunday afternoon would be anything but.

"I know exactly how this is going to shake out," he said, standing up from his seat. "I'm going to spend all day Saturday at a wedding." The ceremony and reception were already on the books. He couldn't get out of it. In fact, he didn't really want to – until this last-minute request showed up. "I can't believe I have to burn up my Sunday working on this ridiculous report!" He was pacing in the living room, marching past the bookshelves, chopping the air with his left hand as he spoke.

"On Friday I'm going to call people and email people and pull information that should be in a database somewhere but we aren't smart enough to operate that way so we will jockey our spreadsheets together. I'm the effing principal at the old school meeting and the work is going to take time and I'm not looking forward to any of it! I know exactly how this is going to go!"

"Really?" the Coach said. "You know how to predict the future?"

The Client wanted to explain himself, but the Coach jumped in before he could open his mouth.

"Do you have a crystal ball? I get that you might have a *feeling* about how this is going to go, how your weekend is going to unfold, but how it's actually going to occur is a complete and utter mystery. Can you see that there are about ten thousand variables that could impact what your actual experience is going to be, starting with the fact that no one can predict the future?"

"I'm just saying," the Client said, looking to win this one, "that I know that the weekend is going to suck!"

"Ah," said the Coach, speeding up his cadence, "Is that an actual fact in the real world, like the fact that water boils at one hundred degrees centigrade, or is 'the weekend is going to suck' a matter of opinion? Has your fate this weekend been predetermined?" His voice was firm, the challenge was clear. The opportunity for defensiveness – or discovery – was encircling the Client.

"How can you know the feelings that will accompany this premonition of yours, unless you are making a decision to manufacture them? Or could it be that your feeling is looking like a rock-solid fact, when really it's just a natural manifestation of a thought?"

Silence.

"I'm listening," was all the Client said.

"I'm not saying you don't know what this weekend *might* look like. I'm not saying you're wrong, or anything like that. But perhaps there's a misunderstanding about how the future actually works. We think it's easier to say, 'I know what's next,' when in reality there's no way we can know exactly what's next. I mean, I don't even know what I'm going to say next. Artichoke hearts. Copernicus. Miley Cyrus. You see what I mean?

"Life is not scripted, no matter how much we want it to be. We say 'I know' to help calm the uncertainty in our minds, especially around a potentially disturbing or uncomfortable situation. But the fact is you have no way of knowing what your experience will be like this weekend, until you go through it. What would happen if you realized that your experience is *never* predetermined? Life doesn't have to suck. You don't have to be sentenced to some horrible fate. What if you don't have to confirm your Sunday feelings by Thursday evening so that you can have seventy-two hours to manifest this emotional disaster area that you're envisioning for yourself? I'm not saying that you can and will enjoy your weekend. Maybe you're right, after all. But there's only one way to find out." The Coach paused. "Look, all I am saying is that there's a way to face the weekend that makes everything . . . "

"More complete?" the Client said. "More . . . predictable? More . . . fulfilling?"

The Coach liked this guy's style. Clearly the Client was a fan of sarcasm. The lines around the Coach's eyes wrinkled again.

"How about *easier*?" the Coach said, shaking his head.

The Client was smiling, too. He wasn't sure if this weekend could get easier. But if there was a way, he had a will to find it.

"Grab that notepad, and let me share some ideas," the Coach said, pointing at the coffee table in front of the Client. "Let's stop trying to predict the future."

The Coach explained that planning wasn't a complete waste of time, but adaptability was always a part of human nature. Like the surfers in the ocean, it's a good idea to wear a wetsuit if it's cold, wax your board, and start at a time when the waves are breaking. "But think about it: should you have a plan for exactly how you are going to surf a wave?" he laughed. "What if the wave has other plans? Best to play it as it comes, because locking in on some well-thought-out plan could land you at the bottom of the ocean."

"What I'm about to share are some tools, not rules, for facing difficult circumstances. For tapping into your deeper nature, when life gets complicated."

"Gotcha," the Client said. He noticed a large painting above the fireplace, a mix of bright reds and blues. It was a child of four or five, but the child had pale blue angel wings and a halo on her head. She appeared to be flying across the canvas. Glancing at the Coach, the Client saw how the angel – undoubtedly the Coach's daughter – shared many of his features.

"Take this moment, right here, right now, not a projection of some future one," the Coach was saying. "Ask yourself this question, about this weekend, or about any difficult circumstance: What else could this mean?

"Working this weekend could mean that your Sunday is going to suck. But what *else* could this mean?"

CHAPTER 11.
CALLING
THE POLICE

I am not this hair,
I am not this skin,

I am the
soul
that lives within.

RUMI
PERSIAN POET & MYSTIC

The Client nodded his head as he considered the question. *What else could this mean?*

He said, "It could mean that I uncover some new possibilities for my company. It could mean that I get one step closer to having the courage to tell them I'm done. It could mean that I don't get to watch the game. It could mean that I take my family out to dinner and tell them how much they mean to me, to make up for lost time together. It could mean a lot of things."

The Coach borrowed the notepad and wrote down two words. "When it comes to difficult times, people are looking for this," he said, pointing to the two words: GET THROUGH. "They want to know how to 'get through' it. In other words, how to cope."

"Right," the Client said. "I'm looking for a way to get through this weekend. And how to get through this dead-end job, so I can find what's next."

"I know that feeling. I know that impulse," the Coach said, glancing at a nearby bookshelf. What did he see there, the Client wondered. The Coach paused.

"When my dad passed away, right in the middle of COVID, I wondered how I was going to get through it."

The Client tilted his head to the left. "I . . . I didn't know. I'm sorry," he said.

"It was a Monday morning when I got a four-word email," the Coach said. "The four words I never wanted to read. 'The test is positive.' What could I do, from five states away?"

"I got him some medicine to make him more comfortable. Ordered it online from a nearby pharmacy. He had been complaining of a lingering cough but never said it was severe. I didn't really notice it, even when we were talking once or twice a week. Didn't seem that bad. Anyway, I got him a virtual appointment with a doctor on Wednesday. He had moved to a new city, so there was some work to be done to get him in front of someone who could help."

"On Wednesday, we were FaceTiming on his laptop. I was going to sit in, virtually, while he talked to the doctor. He gets a phone call from the nurse practitioner: the doctor got called away. She asked him if he could speak with the doctor the next morning, at 11:20 a.m."

The Coach was looking down slightly, speaking of the situation as if he were seeing it on a screen in front of him. Which, as it turns out, he was. "I watch my dad as he tells her, 'Sure, tomorrow morning will be fine.' They hang up their call. I tell him that I'll reach out to him the next morning, a little after 11 a.m., so I can listen in using this same FaceTime arrangement. He agrees. Says it will be great to have another set of eyes and ears on the call. He thanked me for everything.

"That was the last time I spoke to my father," the Coach revealed.

"He never responded to my texts or calls the next morning. I ended up having to ring his apartment complex and ask somebody to knock on his door. No answer. The apartment manager told me, via phone, that they couldn't do anything more at this point. So, from five states away, I called the police. Asked them to go to his apartment. Gave them his address. Told them to do whatever was necessary to reach my dad."

"They found him, unconscious, around noon on Thursday. They revived him. When he was conscious, he couldn't talk or answer questions. The ambulance took him to the hospital just after lunch."

"By Friday at midnight, he was gone."

The Client let out a heavy sigh.

The Coach reached into the bookcase and pulled out a framed photograph. He held it waist high for a moment, looking at it as if he might see something new. Then he passed it over to the Client.

The simple black picture frame held the image of two men, seated at a baseball game. On the left, the Coach was smiling. On his right was an older gent with gray hair and a tan. They didn't necessarily look alike, except for the smile on both of their faces. Behind them, green ballpark seats held the elbows and white cotton jerseys of Astros fans. The guy on the right looked like he was having the time of his life. Beaming, he looked like a kid at a birthday party.

"How old was he?" the Client asked.

"Seventy-seven," the Coach replied. The guy on the right easily looked ten years younger.

"That summer when he passed away . . . " the Coach trailed off. He stopped. Then he found the memory: "Talking with the nurses at the hospital, hearing news of his condition . . . the deterioration . . . there were decisions to be made. I doubled up in pain, like being punched in the gut," the Coach said. "Losing someone, in isolation, being alone with your grief as he was alone with his pain . . . I wouldn't wish that on anyone. And yet, there we were."

The Coach had to handle his father's affairs from a distance. He speculated that his father had been sick with COVID for longer than he let on. His dad was tough, and from a different generation, the Coach explained. His father was not prone to sharing details of his health, because mostly it had been excellent. Until it wasn't.

The Coach explained that his father had donated his body to science. Donation had always been the plan. The doctors refused the body because of COVID-19. An unplanned cremation was arranged, a last-minute solution. There was no formal funeral service.

"My wife and two daughters, we gathered in our living room. Right here. Right here where you are. Five states away from where he passed, we held each other, and we grieved. We lit candles around framed photographs, like the one in your hands. We remembered a life well lived. A life well loved. A man we missed. And we always will.

"I tell you this story to share something I realized. Something I saw, but I didn't want to. Because the way he went . . . " the Coach took a moment to find his thoughts. "I wondered how I was ever going to get through this.

"Somehow, and I don't know where or when or how, a new thought showed up for me. Underneath the waves of grief, I shifted from 'How can I get through this?' I started wondering what I could get *from* this. What would he want me to get from this? The experience, the grief, the surprise, the loss . . . again: what could I get from this? What if I stopped trying to figure it all out, trying to manage my anger and everything, and looked at what I could get from all of this?

"When I shifted from getting *through* to getting *from*, I gained some agency in the situation. I say 'agency' because I didn't gain control. But I gained some ownership. I began to own my experience, not try to manage it, and my relationship to my circumstances started to change."

"I would find myself weeping at a traffic light," the Coach said. "In the midst of these tears, instead of trying to stop the pain or manage the grief, I did nothing. I wasn't passive: in fact, quite the opposite. Because it took some awareness and some effort to stop punishing myself for what I was feeling. Have you been there?" The Client nodded, slowly. He thought of his own parents, both alive and thriving. The Client counted his blessings. But he knew the pain of loss.

"I never wanted to try and cut off the love that I had for the man who raised me, the man who helped me to be who I am today. To try and shut off those feelings would be like trying to cut off my hand or my face. But the grief was . . . rough."

"The love I have for my father," he said, shifting to the present tense, "is something I honor, even now as I share his memory with you. How could my feelings for him be something to deny, or destroy? What would I lose if I tried to manage or modify what I was feeling? The answer is: everything."

The Client wrote the words "Get from" on his notepad.

"Many of my best friends said to me, 'May his memory be a blessing.' The blessing he gave me? I can tell you, that blessing showed up inside of the tears. Inside of the smiles. Smiles, in pictures like the one you are holding, right there. Remembrances of days past. You know how it is. Never, ever will I deny how I felt for my father. His memory is a blessing, and I share it with you today. Because it is his memory that I get from our lifetime together, and what I get from this is what helped me to get through this."

The Client took it all in. As painful as the experience must have been, he saw that his Coach didn't need or want to stop his feelings. Why stifle what was a natural expression of life? Why do we try to plan and control and manage that which is as natural as the waves in the sea? If grief truly was love persevering, who were we to try and stop it?

The wave always comes to you – sometimes in waves of grief. But like that wave, grief can wash over you. Carry you to a new place. A place where you are the same and yet never the same. A place where the Coach was, right now, relaying his story of love persevering. The Client saw that making it okay to grieve was the first step in making it okay to heal. That was what he got from this.

Who was anyone to try and stop the natural flow of life, expressing itself through our laughter and our tears, our frustrations and our fears? Things get easier when we don't have to dominate or medicate our moods. When what we are feeling is the natural extension of our nature, there's nothing to supervise, nothing to sustain, no discipline to maintain.

What the Client got from the Coach's story was a realization. Trying to be predictive of his feelings was . . . what exactly? Perhaps a denial, on some level. A failed attempt at managing or mitigating potential unpleasantness, or recreating happiness, or building some other version of a thought castle inside his imagination. What would happen, he wondered, if he got out of that business? If managing feelings wasn't something he was interested in, what would life feel like?

If he could really embrace the idea that whatever he was feeling was okay, his experience (whatever it was) was going to get easier. If his mood was just a fact of life, not a task to be crossed off a to-do list or an error to be corrected, his relationship to the world around would shift.

"I realized," the Coach said, "that I'm okay inside of every reaction. And so are you. So are we all."

The Coach came and sat down in a chair near the Client. "It's easy to see that we can never know how we will react when we lose someone close to us. We don't know how we will feel when a child is born. We didn't know how we will react when facing a pandemic. In fact, if someone tried to explain those things to us before the experience, the conversation would be meaningless. Incomprehensible. The experience, good, bad, or indifferent, is the fabric of this life. The very human part of our human nature."

"But also, it's crazy to say that we know exactly what the experience will be like this weekend, or on Monday when you go into work, or even next Thursday at lunch when you order the chicken salad. At best we might have a general idea, right? I mean, we've all tried chicken salad so there's that, but the experience of that particular chicken salad, that Thursday chicken salad, is unknown."

"Here's what I'm trying to say," the Coach shared, leaning forward. "*Try that chicken salad.*" He laughed. "Don't think you can taste it right here, right now, inside your mind. Take a big bite. On Thursday. When that bowl of chicken salad is in front of you. Enjoy it. Savor it," he continued, with emphasis. "Live. Your. Life. Stop trying to predict it."

The Client nodded. The Coach continued.

"When my daughter went off to college, I told her one thing: 'Take the ride,' meaning do what you do when you do it. When opportunity shows up, don't waste time talking yourself out of it. You can do almost anything if you won't talk yourself out of it first. I'm talking about the simple decisions that could make her life richer and her experience greater. Like a kid at Disneyland who's curious about a certain ride, but convinces himself that Space Mountain is lousy, or scary, or something reserved for somebody else, not him. He thinks he won't enjoy it. Deep down, maybe he's a little disappointed that he won't go on the ride. But the affirmation of his thinking – 'This ride is no good, I won't enjoy it' – is what he clings to, so that he can be right. Even if it means missing the fun of Space Mountain." The Coach shook his head. "I'm curious: What would you say to that kid?"

"Take the ride," the Client repeated. "If you're lost in your prediction or your speculation, that's not the same as getting the real experience. I wouldn't say it that way to a nine-year-old, but I'd say a version of that. I'd say, you're missing out. Because Space Mountain is awesome."

The Coach nodded. "The map is not the territory," he explained. "What you see on the GPS is not what the trail feels like under your feet, or how the wind sounds when you roll down the window. Take the ride. Stop trying to arrive; just take the ride," the Coach shared. "Shakespeare wrote, 'There is nothing either good or bad in this world but our thinking makes it so.' Stop trying to make it so. Get in line, fasten your seatbelt, experience what life has to offer beyond the way you think about it. Make it okay to feel uncertainty, grief, joy, success, whatever it is that life has on offer. Take the ride!"

The Client was energized by the idea of making it easier to take the ride, whatever that ride might be. And not just because he loved Space Mountain. He was thinking how lucky he was that his own daughters wanted to get on that ride, when they were in Anaheim a few years ago. He still had a little PTSD from riding "It's a Small World" 14 times in a row. However, his little daughter had loved it, so he wasn't going to complain.

"Maybe write this down: *What else could this mean?*" the Coach said, as the Client grabbed the notepad off the coffee table. "These five words will help point toward other possibilities. Here's another: *What's good about this?* You know, you could say that there's nothing good about a funeral, and I wouldn't argue about it, but actually we both know that a funeral is part of the healing process. On the surface it might look unpleasant or undesirable, but when I reflect on the tiny service we had, just my family and me, I can tell you that that was the moment when my healing began. I became closer with my family, with my daughters, with my wife, at our little homemade funeral. We all spoke. We all shared. We all saw what my father meant to us."

"He must have been an amazing man," the Client said.

"He was," the Coach agreed, with a smile that mirrored the image in the photograph. "He was."

The Client was considering what to write down, when the Coach spoke again. "We don't own the future," he said. "So there's no need to manage it." He excused himself, to give the Client time to write down what had stood out for him, as their day came to a close.

21. Stop trying to predict the future = Easier.

22. Stop trying to arrive. Just take the ride.

23. What else could this mean? (Is there an easier point of view)?

24. What's good about this? Goodness can make things easier!

25. What can I get from this?

26. What if we don't need to manage our feelings? Easier.

27. What if memories are a blessing, not something to be managed?

28. Denying your feelings is unnecessary.

29. Grief can be a gift.

30. When you try the chicken salad, really REALLY try the chicken salad.

CHAPTER 12.
THE HAIL MARY

today having power

means
knowing
what to ignore.

YUVAL NOAH HARARI
ISRAELI SOCIAL SCIENTIST AND AUTHOR,'HOMO DEUS'

Three days later, at 4:40 p.m. on Sunday afternoon, the Coach's phone rang. He was walking into the house, back from a quick trip to the store. The FaceTime call was from the Client. Quickly, the Coach entered the house and set the grocery bag on the kitchen counter while his thumb responded to the call. "Hey there!" he said, looking at the screen, "I didn't expect to hear from you so soon. How was your weekend?"

On the screen, the Client was grinning from ear to ear. "I did it. I really did it!"

The Coach asked if he had quit his job.

"No, not yet. Nothing like that! I have had the most amazing weekend – you're not going to believe it." The Client was sitting at his kitchen table. The background of white walls behind him was a simple frame for the FaceTime conversation.

The Client relayed a story of how he recognized that the layers of thinking around this last-minute request were suffocating him. If infinite creativity were always available, he reasoned, why wasn't he able to tap into it? If he were wired and built to adapt and really operated inside of a universe that had his back, why couldn't he see it?

"Well, new ideas are always available, except for my thinking," he said. "My concentration on the utter hassle of this redundant assignment was just filling me up with so much . . . anger! So much indignation! And when I found myself getting frustrated . . . " his voice trailed off.

"What did you do?" the Coach interjected. He was putting some blueberries into the refrigerator while he held the phone in his left hand at arm's length.

The Client was on a roll. "I found *myself.* I found that I was more than my thinking, my feelings of being wronged, or inconvenienced, or hassled or whatever. We were going to the wedding – my wife agreed to drive, which was a huge help, and we were talking about my frustration in the car. My girls were in the back seat, and as I was going on and on about how I had already done this work before, my ten-year-old says, 'Dad, they ask us to do the same problems over and over in math class. Why can't you just do the problem again?'"

"What did you make of that?" the Coach inquired.

"Well, I was creating this massive story of injustice and repetition and just all kinds of head trash and my kid just simplified the whole thing for me. I decided to drop my story."

"How did you do that, exactly?" The Coach was really curious.

"I didn't do anything! It's what I *stopped* doing that made everything easier," the Client explained. "Sometimes kids can see things in a way that is so much purer than the way we process stuff. They come from a much more natural state. Really just . . . honest, you know what I mean? And from this natural state, she was saying, just do the deal, Dad – do what your boss is asking you to do. I didn't try to control the story, or rewrite it, or manage my emotions around it. I was still pissed off that I was being robbed of my Sunday, but I saw that impulse for what it was: just a thought."

The Client was on the move, headed through his own house, past pictures of his family. He was in his own living room now, and the Coach saw beautiful abstract artwork that bordered floating shelves behind the Client's head. He wondered if one or both of the Client's daughters would make an appearance.

"It's amazing what you can accomplish when you just drop the color commentary. Like dropping commas. Putting in more periods. Stuff gets simpler. The elaboration stops and the management of moods just seems to slip away! I mean, I wasn't

in some Zen-like state of constant euphoria. But recognizing
that I was having some thinking about the work allowed me to
also recognize that those thoughts were just part of my
experience. When I got okay with how I was feeling, when my
experience of frustration wasn't something I needed to manage,
fix, or control, I was able to do something really cool."

"And what was that?" the Coach said.

"Take action! Lots and lots of action. I changed my . . . okay,
I don't know how I did this, but I changed my relationship with
my work. I don't even know if it was me that did it. It just kinda
happened! My identity went from 'angry frustrated guy in a
dead-end job burning through the weekend' to something
different." He paused to gather his next thought. "I was focused
on the task at hand – almost like the work was coming through
me. When I moved from taking things personally to just taking
things as they came, one idea after the other . . . well, my work
accelerated in a way that was absolutely crazy."

"It's funny," the Coach said, "Speeding up happens fast,
when you start in neutral." The Coach decided to walk out of
the house and enter the back patio. A light rain was falling, but
he was covered and dry. He sat down at one of the chairs where
he had met with the client just a few days before. He perched
the phone up against a flowerpot on a nearby table.

The Client jumped in, "I found some new ideas for
investment," he explained, offering details on how the company
might acquire new capabilities, even when revenues were down.
He did a detailed cash-flow analysis of one of the company's
smaller competitors, showing how the acquisition would pay for
itself. The net effect was a cash-flow purchase that allowed them
to buy a missing technology, with a payback period of less than
21 months. He didn't know if the CEO would go for it, but also
–he didn't care. He was, he said, detached from the outcome.

His life wasn't defined by the terms inside the report, the history of the company, or the projections of his team. His identity was separate from his work, he said, and he truly saw it. He saw that possibilities existed.

When he stopped thinking about how he was living, he really started to live.

To do.

To thrive.

He was looking toward the infinite, toward creativity, instead of trying to solve and correct himself, his career, his boss, or really, anything. His identity wasn't even a consideration; he was just a man in motion, moving through reports and riding the waves to see what showed up next.

When he stopped trying to correct anything, he said, he accessed everything. It was like playing piano, but the song only contained 10 notes – the 10 piano keys he could touch. Imagine thinking that you could only play the 10 keys underneath your fingers, as if your hands were fixed and your wrists were frozen and you couldn't even spread out your fingers or move your hands to access different keys! The Client laughed at the thought. Inside the laughter, he saw it: he could always access every key on the piano. Even though he only had 10 fingers, he could move around and touch any and every key – and there were 88 possibilities there. He liked that point of view. He zoomed out to see it.

He stopped trying to manage the future. As a result, he found himself in the present. Putting together information and projections and connections in ways that he hadn't experienced before, he felt flexibility inside of what originally seemed like the most backward, rigid, and redundant assignment he had ever encountered in his nearly 10 years with the firm.

He said he didn't care if things didn't turn out the way he planned or projected. His projections were impersonal, but supportive, like the universe around him. His report allowed for uncertainty, and so did he – without any discomfort whatsoever. The work he completed today wasn't an exercise in trying to fix the unfixable or change the minds of anyone who might read his report.

"Do the doable," the Client said, "and I did."

He realized that insights had come to him. He didn't have to manufacture them. Like clouds in the sky, those insights showed up, more easily than ever before. Like waves in the sea, the ideas came to him.

The Client noted that the request was still not a source of delight for him. But, while the request remained the same, he had changed his relationship with the ask. With the deadline. With the requirements.

His relationship to his work had changed. Transformed. Even though his job was still the same, the way he related to it made everything different. The Coach congratulated him on his exceptional progress and encouraged him to go further. "Say more," he prodded.

He was A-OK with his reaction to his circumstance – with his humanity – mentioning how anybody would be angry if they had to deal with this kind of stupidity. Nobody likes to burn up a Sunday! But instead of fury, he was laughing. Laughing! Nothing had really changed, but he was different.

"What if it's not on me to solve a problem or think my way into some kind of solution," he asked the Coach rhetorically. What if when he had an angry reaction or he felt frustrated or whatever, he didn't have to resolve that thought, or modify it in any way? "The idea that the universe might help me out really resonated," he said. "And the wave came to me."

The Client zoomed out. He let himself just be. Be angry. Be irritated. Be productive. Whatever. It was all okay with him. When he wasn't on his mind, he was doing what needed to be done. Instead of becoming a constant gardener for a made-up stream of consciousness, he tapped into a place of connection. And when he did, a new identity bloomed.

Suddenly, an adorable dark-haired girl of about six or seven years old came into frame, wrapping her arms around the Client's neck and pushing her face into his. Her hair was rumpled and straight and she had white barrettes on either side of her forehead so that she could see and be seen. She was wearing an evening gown, dressed as a character from *Frozen*. She mumbled something inaudible into his ear and the Client laughed.

He pulled back to look at her. He realized he was the guy who got a ton of stuff done on a Sunday afternoon, without giving up anything. Because, right here and right now, he had everything. He rubbed noses with his daughter and told her that he was on a call. So the little girl turned her face to the Coach and said hello. Then she darted out of frame before he could reply.

The Coach was smiling deeply at the little exchange inside the FaceTime call. He offered words of encouragement, to reinforce what the Client was already seeing. "What else can you invite, from the infinite, into your life?" he wondered.

"What, indeed," the Client said, considering the possibilities. "I've already sent the report to the CEO," he said, "and I just had to share the news with you. Now I'm going to take my family out to dinner, to celebrate!"

The Coach was pleased to see the Client's progress and told him so. Inspired by their work together, the Client felt certain that he could move forward with his resignation sometime in the next month or two. They agreed to speak later in the week, and the Coach congratulated him once again on his progress around the report.

Currently, that report was being used to sharpen an axe. Soon that axe would strike a fatal blow to the Client's career.

In 16 hours, he would be fired from his job.

CHAPTER 13.
TO THE GALLOWS

It seems impossible

until it's
done.

NELSON MANDELA
PRESIDENT OF SOUTH AFRICA

Traffic on the Dallas North Tollway moved at the speed of
business. Cement barriers cradled the cars as the Monday
morning traffic moved with purpose if not speed. A radio station
that only plays what they want threw together a set of Los Lonely
Boys, Dua Lipa, and Bruno Mars. The Client's car was full of
music, with a triple play that easily coaxed a musical response out of
him. Absent of much thought, the songs – each super-catchy –
landed on his ears in a new way. He noticed that he was really
enjoying the music. Sending in the report last night had given him
a new lease on life. However, that lease – in terms of his career –
would be up in 32 minutes. Renewal would not be an option.
Dripping in "Finesse," the Client gripped the wheel at ten and two.

His office was an enormous metallic glass skyscraper. The
building was a supermodel, looking down on the nearby retail
shops as if they were junior high cheerleaders. The Legacy West
area in Plano always seemed like a coloring book to him.
Something in the mixed-used development felt incomplete.
He wasn't an architect, and they weren't paying him to fix the
landscaping, but the whole picture hadn't really come together yet.
Like most of North Dallas, this manufactured patch of the world
was covered in the fingerprints of man, not necessarily the hand of
God. Perhaps in time it would feel more colored in, he reasoned.

The snazzy glass tower sat on tan roads between trendy
shops bordered by parched grass in a nearby field, a study in
ecru and engineering. He parked in the garage. Grabbing his
backpack, he walked toward the double doors. There he was met
by the Chief Human Resources Officer less than eight minutes
before he got some very bad news.

"How's it going?" he said, appreciating that she was holding the door open for him. Last year, she had helped him to bring on two new recruits and transfer a problem employee into another division. Her hair was pulled back in a bun. She wore a tailored blue business suit. In her left arm she clutched a leather portfolio to her chest.

She adjusted her glasses as he approached. He smiled at her while she pulled at her lapel and looked down to her right at absolutely nothing. "Hi, good morning," she said.

She followed him inside and asked him, from behind, if he had a minute. He turned back over his shoulder.

At this company, he had exactly seven minutes.

"Let's grab a spot in the first-floor conference room," she said, matching his pace and then quickening her own. She opened the meeting room door for him again. He appreciated the courtesy.

As he entered the room and stepped to the left, she followed him like a shadow, then broke quickly to the right. He turned to look at what she was doing. Why was she in a hurry? He adjusted his backpack from shoulder to hand.

Before one could say, "Is that axe for me?" she touched a button near the door. The clear glass was already opaque, now it became a solid sheet of white, cloaking their meeting in complete privacy. The Client turned into the room to find a seat.

At the large conference table, a gaunt man in a dark suit was writing on a legal pad. The Client recognized the bony fingers and patchwork beard of the company's chief legal counsel. Closing the notebook, the hired hand from one of the larger corporate law firms in North Dallas looked up.

The door closed with a solid thud.

"Please, have a seat," said the woman in the blue suit. The Client's spider sense was tingling.

He tossed down his backpack on the floor next to a leather chair. An open laptop sat in the middle of the conference table.

The CHRO spun the laptop so that the screen faced him. "Okay," was all she said.

On the laptop, a Zoom call was active.

The scene on the screen was serene. An angular wooden deck, blonde and glowing in the sun, formed the bottom of a frame for a beautiful lake. An expensive patio chair sat askew in the middle of the lakefront vista, butting up against some sort of picnic table where a laptop was revealing the aforementioned scenery. Wispy clouds splashed across the vast sky.

"I'm back. Sorry I'm late," the CEO said, off camera. "Thanks for coming."

She entered stage left and took her position in the chair. She centered herself midframe and started futzing with the angle of the screen. "Can you guys hear me okay?"

Soon the Client would wish he couldn't.

From her lake house, the CEO cut right to the chase. She didn't have a lot of time for this meeting, but the subject was important. And difficult. She hoped he would understand.

Understand what?

They had worked together for a couple of years. The CEO was part of new management, brought in to revitalize the company. Unfortunately, her results did anything but. Her background was finance; she had been CFO at an investment firm before she was moved into the top spot at the Client's company. When the old CEO retired, there was a changing of the guard. The Client was unfazed by the transition.

He was a professional, seven years at the firm at the time. He appreciated her knowledge of operations, and her attention to the numbers. Speaking of numbers, his last performance review was excellent. The positive feedback had built a bond between them. However, "bond" might be a stretch. The whole relationship felt more like appreciation, nothing more.

The CEO had come to trust him. Not as part of her inner circle. But he was one of the chief lieutenants who could marshal the troops and lead a charge when needed.

The CEO's attention to the company's performance was thorough, and intricate. The Client always wondered why she seemed to lack imagination when it came to his ideas. Growth strategies were never really of interest to her, especially if there were investments to be made. On the one hand, he admired her fiscally conservative approach to profitability. On the other, he wondered how the company could save to growth.

Their relationship was never contentious, but he didn't win a lot. She was often grateful; that was as close as he came to praise. However, his proposals always landed with a thud. Like the sound of the massive, closed door on the conference room.

The Client never met a request for work he didn't like. Oh, he may not have liked the implications of the request, or the timing, or even the way he was asked. But he was not the kind of guy to say no to a direct order or a to-do. "No" was a sign of defeat. You figure it out, he told himself, just as his parents, teachers, and athletic coaches had told him in some form or fashion his whole life. And so far, he had.

He was in the "get-it-done" business, even if it meant burning up a weekend. The good news, as he saw it, was how he discovered a new relationship within that weekend. Actually, he wasn't sure how, or even if he was the one who discovered it. Like the South Pole, was it always there? But that didn't really matter, because the task got done and he felt good about it.

The most he could do for the CEO, he knew, was what he was asked. His ideas and extra innovations were never received in the same spirit they were given. He had presented multiple business plans, hiring strategies, even the most recent acquisition strategy, always outlining ideas for advancement and growth. Strategic recommendations, he knew, wouldn't really fly.

Or did he? Did he know? The conversation with the Coach had introduced a comfort with uncertainty. He was trying to get out of the future-predicting business. The conversation last week had encouraged him to stop trying to manufacture assumptions. Perhaps the CEO saw something in the report that was intriguing? Maybe the lawyer was here to talk about what that acquisition could look like, or to suss out some of the finer details in the report? His career was definitely at a turning point. Just in the exact opposite way he imagined.

"What's up?" he said. "Was there something wrong with the report?"

No, the CEO explained. "We aren't here to discuss the report." She thanked him for his hard work over the weekend. She praised his work. She told him how much she appreciated his contribution.

However, she said, as the other shoe began to drop, his division had been sold. Investment bankers. The buyers wanted to run the business with a skeleton crew, and their own people. They wanted to squeeze whatever profits they could out of the existing business. "I have to inform you," she said in an even and clear tone that matched the way she had been rehearsing it in the guest bathroom of her 4,000-square-foot house on Lake Texoma, "We need to end your employment with the company, effective immediately."

When your head is severed from your body, you don't feel a thing. Because not only are your nerves and spinal cord sliced in two, but you are also dead.

The Client experienced a silence like the void of space. Everything slowed way, way, way down.

He blinked at the screen. He looked over at the exploratory beard that had uncertain plans for the lawyer's neck. The CHRO was staring at the conference table, witnessing the show in silence. The door was still shut, and he had no idea when it might open again.

His eyes made their way back to the screen. "Sold the division?" was all he could manage. Then his brain kicked back on: "There's a way to bring this division back to life, didn't you see in the . . . " he stopped. He took a breath. He knew better than to fight or argue. "I'm guessing this decision has been made."

"Correct," the CEO said. "You are being informed. This is a conversation. Not a debate." She outlined the perfunctory steps of his termination. She could not see the CHRO or the lawyer, but clearly she knew they were in the room, and referred to their roles in the process.

The lawyer got the hint, grabbed the touchpad with his skeletal fingers, and turned on the big screen TV. Another few taps from his needly digits and the video call went to the big screen, activating the conference room camera underneath the giant Samsung.

When the CEO's lake house was on the television, the CHRO stood up, leaned across the table, and shut the laptop. The Client once again had no choice. He turned to his left to face the main camera and screen, kicking over his backpack in the process. He let it sit there on the floor.

Intent on the screen and nothing else, the Client said directly to the CEO, "I can't believe this. You just gave me a good review! Why can't you find a spot for me somewhere else in the company?"

"Well," the CEO began, "the thing is . . . " Her lips kept moving but the audio was gone.

The Client looked to the right, and he saw the CHRO holding the clicker like a phaser, pointed at the screen. Her left thumb was perched atop the mute button. The CHRO knew what the CEO forgot: namely, that reasons and rebuttals were not appropriate in a firing. Whatever the CEO might say could be used against her if this business decision turned into a legal matter. Especially if she indicated that they had thought twice about the firing, because saying too much would be opening

Pandora's box. There was nothing to explain or defend, as she had mentioned to the CEO during their dress rehearsal earlier that morning. Emotions were unwelcome, information was the only goal. When they reviewed their roles without the Client in the room, everyone was clear. But in the heat of the moment, the CEO had decided to offer a potentially risky explanation. Which, when the audio was cut, no one ever heard.

The CHRO spoke to everyone in a clear and even tone. "We are not prepared to discuss that right now," she said, still not ready to lift a finger to help the Client's career. Looking to the TV at the front of the room, everyone saw that the CEO's mouth had become a thin and motionless line. Satisfied with the silence, the CHRO released the mute button.

The attorney, who struggled to find a shirt with a collar small enough to fit his wiry neck while accommodating his mantis-like arms, pulled a manila envelope from beneath his closed portfolio. His Adam's apple looked like a baby's fist trying to punch through a pink blanket covered with patchy bits of dark brown hair. The baby's fist twisted and struggled for freedom as the lawyer spoke.

"The terms of your severance are included in this package," he said, his voice deep and clear. He was holding the manila envelope but not ready to slide it across the table just yet. "The terms will be given to you as you leave today. Please review the contents and return it by the due date. You may wish to have someone examine it, as that is your right."

The loose-fitting shirt collar swung beneath his vocal production mechanism, supporting an expensive tie that was both overly formal for the situation and just right for the image the lawyer wanted to project.

The Client was encouraged to look over the terms inside the envelope. But not in the room. Because they were not prepared to discuss that right now.

Given his current state of mind, neither was he.

The CHRO said something about getting back to them in two weeks regarding how he planned to move forward. His email had been shut down. His file access blocked. His cell phone was his, not the company's, so that still worked. He would leave the building and come back next week to get his things. He was cautioned verbally in the room: do nothing to disparage the company, either verbally or online. Doing so would void the severance package. He understood the restrictions. Anything else?

He would be escorted out once they were done. "Did you need anything, any medications or anything, from your desk? I can go and get it for you, before you leave," the CHRO said.

The CEO watched it all with apparent disinterest from the 75-inch screen.

Satisfied that no one other than her had botched their lines in their six-minute play, she chimed in. "Okay, I gotta run. You're in good hands with these two. Best of luck to you in your future endeavors." The big screen went black.

The Client was left with two of his co-workers. His peers. No, strike that – his *former* peers. He was sitting across from an attorney. Did he need one?

He stood up and grabbed his backpack with his left hand. The lawyer stood up as well, handing over the brown envelope. The Client slid the terms of separation into a large half-zipped pocket as he walked to the door. He twisted the doorknob with his free hand and pushed. The door didn't budge. He pushed again. Once more, and this time he leaned into it. Nothing. He stood up straight and huffed out a sigh.

He realized that the door opened to the inside.

"Who the hell," the Client said to no one in particular, "fires somebody first thing Monday morning?"

CHAPTER 14.
LIFE AFTER DEATH

never confuse
a single defeat

with
a final defeat.

F. SCOTT FITZGERALD
AUTHOR OF 'THE GREAT GATSBY'

The next thing the Client knew, he was sitting in his car. He was smacking the steering wheel; how many times, he didn't know. When the palm of his hand started to sting, he stopped. He remembered that the SUV lease was three months old – a financial obligation that he now had no paycheck to support. Nice. Smart. Great timing. His hand wasn't the only thing that stung.

He smacked the wheel once again. Why did I do that, he wondered. Nothing made sense. Nothing was going as planned, including the throbbing at the base of his thumb.

They beat me to it, the Client thought to himself. I wanted to leave but they pushed me out. Bagged, tagged, and gagged. He sat back in the seat, unable to start the car because he didn't know where to go. His thoughts went to his wife. How could he tell her what had just happened? What about his daughters? The lower-school semester would be over soon. That private school tuition, times two, wasn't going to take care of itself. Where would that money come from? His wife had her business, but they shared the household expenses. Two salaries were needed to keep the boat afloat.

Considering his lost paycheck, he had a sinking feeling.

What would his wife do, or say, or think of him? He started the car. He didn't know where he was going but he needed to drive. Needed to get out of that parking garage. Needed to distance himself from his former employer.

The post-rush-hour traffic was light, and before he knew it, he was on the other side of the airport. The only thing going faster than the cars around him was his mind.

He was beaten. Robbed. Powerless. He found himself, two hours later, cruising in the general direction of his neighborhood. Along the journey, he had played out the conversation with his wife 397 times in his head, finally deciding to go for an even 400 before pulling into his own driveway. His imagination was running his personal version of the movie *Groundhog Day*.

Turning off the engine, he realized he had gone through nearly every possible scenario: divorce, separation, high anxiety, stomach ulcers, a Xanax addiction, humiliation, mistrust, and disgust. His wife would bail out, taking the kids; he was sure of it. She was brilliant, beautiful, capable, and successful. She deserved better. She couldn't count on him. He couldn't count on himself. But who was counting?

He was damaged goods. Returned without a refund. His former company had been gutted like a fish; he was a discarded bone. His unimaginative CEO had used her imagination (and his detailed reporting) to sell the company to the investors just the way they wanted it: namely, without him in it.

Sitting in his garage, he wondered if he had heard all of the conversation that had taken place in the conference room. Details on the severance package were fuzzy, as well as timelines and even how he would return his laptop. They hadn't confiscated anything in the meeting, and he had a bunch of files at home that would probably be useful to the new ownership. He thought they said his team had been fired as well. Or that they would be? Why hadn't they told him about that? Or had they, and he was too preoccupied with the lawyer's knuckles and patchwork beard to really consider what was discussed?

At some point, he decided the speculation about his impending divorce wasn't getting any better inside his car. Time to go in, say what happened, and face the music.

His wife was cleaning up a broken dish when he entered the kitchen. "Well, hello there," she said, from a kneeling position near the sink. She stood up and placed a dustpan filled with blue ceramic chunks on the counter. "You're home early!"

He told her everything.

"They beat me to it," he said. She knew he had wanted to leave the company for a very long time.

"They got me. The division was cut to the bone and sold. I'm done."

She came to him and touched his face with one hand, and then two, cupping his chin between them. She pulled him closer, leaning in on her tiptoes, and kissed him ever so softly on the mouth. He shut his eyes and wondered if he deserved that kiss. If he deserved her.

She shut her eyes. Every ounce of her being was full of gratitude. At last, she thought. We have everything we need.

Her almond eyes looked up at him, with the tiniest of tears coming to rest inside her bottom lashes. Her skin, impossibly beautiful from any angle or distance, caught the light perfectly without effort or intention. He loved her deeply, and wanted to take care of her – not because of some antiquated gender ritual or outdated family concept; he simply wanted to give this woman what he believed she deserved. Which was, in a word, everything. But how could you give someone that which you had lost, that which you had not, that which had been taken from you?

"Oh," she said, her brown eyes darting ever so slightly as she looked up at him. He was bracing for impact, the scolding that would begin with her deep disappointment, leading to the imminent logical and well-deserved conclusion that separation, and ultimately divorce, was what he really deserved. After all, if his job was gone, how could she stay?

How could she leave? His wife saw a man who wasn't broken.

Did the change in his employment happen in the exact way that he wanted? She didn't care. Victory was his – and theirs. All was not lost. Everything was gained. They were together. What more did they need?

Would they be able to step into the simple pleasures of life, somehow, and embrace what he had been given? She knew the answer was yes. She couldn't wait to find out what that world would be like. The barrier that was keeping them apart was finally removed. That barrier had been keeping her husband from himself, and by extension, from her.

She saw the diligence in this man. He tried so hard. He worked hard. Wanted to do more. Be more. Achieve more. She knew he had hired a coach. The investment was money well spent. Her husband wanted to break free from his professional prison. Why not get some help, she reasoned.

They talked about the experience of his time in Austin. She was encouraged with feelings of progress and knew that he would be able to make a change in his career. The break didn't go as planned, but he was out, nonetheless. The change he had wanted – the change she had wanted – had happened.

Looking into his eyes, she saw the tears he was fighting to contain. His tears were trapped behind his eyes, kept back by that same fighting spirit that held him back in his job. She cried for him, the tears he would not allow himself to shed. But her tears were tears of joy.

At last, he was returned to her. A dark spot was removed. They had been separated by his work. Now they were reunited.

She held both his hands. A shiny gold and silver wedding band rested on his third finger. Did he know that his ring would always be her favorite piece of jewelry?

Supporting his hands, she spoke. "You are free." And then, lifting her eyes to his, "You. Are. Free." She hugged him close and whispered in his ear. "Look at us! We are okay. You are okay. Oh my God," she said, pulling back to look at his face. "Thank God that's over."

And she laughed.

Before he knew what was happening, so did he. They held each other in a deep embrace, hugging and laughing. They shared the same breath.

His career was imploding. But he was not.

The dishes were broken. But he was fine.

His wife saw that everything was not only okay – everything was just right.

Soon, she knew he would feel something he hadn't felt for a very long time. Because, inside of the tears in his shining blue eyes, she saw it.

Hope.

There is always hope.

She had been holding on to it for so long, and all she wanted to do was to give it to him. She didn't know how. She struggled to find a way to let him see who he was. To tell him of the universe she saw inside of him. To help him find the freedom that, today, this morning, was finally his. And hers. And theirs.

"This is the absolute best thing that could have happened to us," his wife said, wiping away a tear. He laughed even harder. She shouted, "It's a gift!"

In the middle of awful circumstances, and what looked like the greatest defeat of his life and career, the Client was held. Supported. Surrounded by nothing less than love.

In his wife's smile, he was more than his career. Much more.

He didn't know if the universe had his back, but he could feel his wife's hands there. Which was close enough for him. He glanced at the dustpan. Jagged pieces of what was once a blue dinner plate were piled on top of each other.

His wife always picked up the pieces.

He was so worried about supporting her. Then he realized that she was supporting him.

Perhaps that's how love works?

Where he imagined disappointment, he found joy. When he stepped outside of the story inside his head, he saw the natural state around him. Namely, he knew that he was loved.
He *was* love.

Not a corporate castaway. Not a failed foot soldier. Not a discarded fish bone.

Standing next to the kitchen island, beside the dishwasher, six feet from the microwave, an idea started to sink in.

He was okay.

He thought of the Kurt Vonnegut quote from his book of the same name: "If this isn't nice, what is?"[1]

He had everything he needed. What more could he ask for, in this moment, right here and right now?

His thinking settled down.

He and his wife sat down at the round white breakfast table in the kitchen. She asked him about how it all shook out.
A wave of curiosity overtook the room. "How," she wondered, "did they do you this favor? What did they say? What was the experience like for you?"

In his recollection of the meeting, there were gaps in his memory. In the closed-door meeting, he had filled those gaps with anger, frustration, indignation, disappointment, and other versions of punishing self-talk. He also included some misdirected seething at the poor skinny-suited bastard who was just trying to do his job and share some important legal details, which the Client still had not been able to consider or digest.

Like a scene in a movie, everyone had their roles to play. He couldn't see the scene, because he was inside it. Wrapped up in his own personal turmoil. But time, space, and distance brought him some clarity. The storm had passed. He zoomed out.

Inside the conference room, the voice inside the Client's head had drowned out the words of the other players in the scene – the other three people who, quite frankly, were there to help him with his transition.

"What was the mood in the room?" his wife wanted to know. She got up for a glass of water and returned with two.

From the kitchen table, instead of the conference table, realizations popped up all over the place. He saw that there was nothing sinister in their morning conversation. A business decision had been made. He was informed of the decision. He had some decisions to make himself. The first one? He had decided not to listen.

He took a drink of water.

Companies get bought and sold all the time. He had not been consulted on the decision. But that consultation was not part of his job description. So why was it part of his expectation?

His Coach would say that he was making the impersonal personal. And the Coach would also say that taking things personally was perfectly normal. How could someone not take the disintegration of their company (and, potentially, their livelihood) personally? Somebody pulls away the career you've held for a decade, you're going to have some thinking around the transition. Who wouldn't?

The Client started to see that the firing was both impersonal and personal. There it was again: "both, and." The universe was just doing its thing while he was doing his. Namely, being a human being, in the middle of being fired. As a result of the conference room gathering, he had enough head trash to propel him around the airport before he made his way home.

At the kitchen table, he made another executive decision. He decided not to beat himself up for the way the meeting went down. He decided that not listening wasn't yet another misstep in a career marked by errors and failures, but a natural reaction to an unexpected conversation. He embraced the idea of being okay, and those thoughts of insufficiency slid past his identity. He didn't need to engage.

It was a choice that was as simple as looking out the window instead of looking at the stove. Effortless. He recognized that he had some thinking around the situation. And, for a change, he let that shit go. He didn't try to manage his thoughts or assess his behavior or create a mental spreadsheet around his potential liabilities.

He had a different identity now. He didn't build it, reach for it, imagine it, or believe in it. He was "both, and."

In retrospect, the conference room dialogue was neutral. Reasonable. He was not.

So what, he wondered? A new viewpoint emerged: the CEO was simply selling an unprofitable business in the way that made sense to her, and her buyers.

The CEO had been building the company for sale, not for growth. No doubt she had connections with an appetite for acquisition. She had done her job. She had sacrificed his. The choice wasn't malicious. It was business. If he were in her shoes, he realized, he would have done the same thing.

And why did he care that she was calling in from the lake house? At least she had the guts and the conscience to face him, via Zoom, and look him in the eye as they parted ways.

His resentment relented.

His misplaced anger loosened its hold on his head and his heart. Gratitude was a bridge too far. But somehow his anger was diffusing.

Later he would realize that he did nothing to shift his state of mind from epic indignation to far-reaching clarity in the course of just a few hours. The change – the adaptation, the transformation – happened all on its own.

Like the tree growing outside his kitchen window, growth was almost imperceptible. Yet change was happening nonetheless. He didn't need to concentrate on his mindset, or find grit, willpower, or some dime-store psychology to control his mood and force a new perspective into his brain. "When in doubt, wait it out."

His brain was already wired and ready for a new thought. That was how the system was designed.

By leaving his thinking alone, new thoughts showed up. Like leaves on a tree. He was reminded of his Coach's voice, saying, "That's how thought works. But only one hundred percent of the time."

He turned his head to the left, and saw his backpack sitting in its favorite chair. He must have dropped it there, entering the house with the same reflex that happened every time he came home from the office. The corner of a brown manila envelope peeked out of a half-opened zippered pocket. "Let me dig into this written stuff," he said to his wife, "and then we can talk some more."

Note

1. Vonnegut, Kurt, *If This Isn't Nice, What Is?* (Seven Stories Press, 2013).

CHAPTER 15.
FINANCIAL
MATTERS

Embrace the unpredictable and unexpected.

It is the path to the infinitely creative in you.

DEEPAK CHOPRA
AUTHOR AND PHILOSOPHER

The next day, the Client found himself in his home office. The Pandemic Palace, his wife called it. He sat, staring at the familiar desk and camera, crowned by the ring light that rarely got used anymore.

He had just read through the terms of the separation agreement when his phone chirped.

He looked down to see a text message from the Coach.

In a second a picture came through via text:

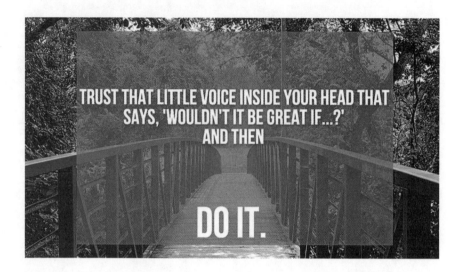

The Client started to text, then stopped and hit the
call button.

When the Coach picked up, he said, "I need your help."

With his elbows on the desk and the phone cupped to his
face, the Client related all recent events. The Coach listened.

"Now I've just reviewed the severance package," the Client
said, "and I am not sure what to do. They gave me eight weeks'
salary and three months of insurance benefits. After nearly ten
years with the firm!" The Coach suspected it was more like eight or
nine years, tops. After some gentle prodding, the Client confessed
that it was nine years and one month. A week for every year of
service was standard issue; some might even call it generous, when
a company was sold. After all, there was no law requiring any kind
of severance package that resembled what he had received.

So, eight weeks. The Coach wondered if the Client saw it as
a gift, or a slap?

The response to that question took about 25 minutes, as the Client recounted what he had done for the firm over the last nine (not ten) years.

The Coach listened intently. When the Client came to a stopping place, the Coach asked, "Do you have any vacation time coming your way?"

The Client realized that he did. He had skimmed the document, finding only what he was looking for (the amount of severance) instead of looking over the whole package. The Coach wasn't an HR expert or some sort of severance wizard. He just knew how to zoom out.

The four weeks' vacation pay, which the company had no doubt calculated, brought his severance package to 12 weeks. The Client found that math articulated on the eleventh page of the 13-page document he received. In an instant, the package went from punitive to more than fair. But where was the Client's mood? Did it improve with the discovery of an extra month's salary? Were things getting easier?

Instead of being thrilled, the Client was stunned. And angry.

How could he be so stupid as to forget about his vacation pay? He often read reports with an exceptional attention to detail. Why not this one?

He had been working on a budgetary spreadsheet, figuring out his finances, to see what he would need to do to survive. Circumstances, in his mind, were dire. The spreadsheet, and the severance package, told a different story. But the Client was not in the mood to be confused by the facts.

He was convinced he would not have enough to make it to the holidays. He was convinced his possibilities were limited, and his reading of the severance package manifested his limited perspective.

"That's how limited perspectives work," the Coach said. "They don't really allow you to see anything else other than what you want to see. The good news is you want to see something more. And there is still more to see."

"I just want to know," the Client said, "that we are going to be safe and comfortable."

"What would make you safe, and comfortable?" the Coach asked the Client. The Client began describing some of the high-level details of his budget, starting with a regression analysis on December spending. As he dove into the interest rate on his mortgage, the Coach cut him off.

"Let me ask you," the Coach said, apologizing for the interruption, "what would you do, right now, if you knew you were safe and comfortable?" Inner knowing was more powerful than outer spreadsheets, the Coach knew. But the Client hadn't discovered that fact.

The Client paused.

He considered the Coach's construct as a hypothetical. "If you had a unicorn, what would you feed it? Assuming you sprouted wings from your shoulder blades, where would you fly?"

The Coach asked him to stop and really consider what the world would look like if he had everything he needed. "Would you be open to some guidance?" he asked the Client. Seeing the head nod, he continued. "Two words. Two words that need to be spoken into this conversation. These two words will help you with every aspect of your life. Two words that will make this conversation easier. Here they are: *slow down*."

"But my spreadsheet shows that in February of next year, we are going to be facing . . . " The Coach cut him off. He knew the Client's analytical skills were formidable, and powerful. He also knew that the Client was using that power against himself. "*Slow down*," the Coach said again.

"When February gets here, *you will figure it out.*"

The Client wasn't sure.

"What are you going to have for lunch tomorrow?" the Coach asked him, out of nowhere.

The Client quickly said, "I have no idea."

"Aren't you worried about that? Tomorrow, high noon. You're going to have a decision to make," he said to the Client.

"That's ridiculous. When tomorrow gets here I'll figure it out."

The phone line was silent. The Coach waited.

The Client made the discovery.

Feeling safe was a state of mind. Not an external circumstance. Safety and comfort, along with every other state of mind ever in the history of humankind, always comes from one place, and one place only: the inside.

Planning could be valuable; the Coach didn't deny the utility. But if your state of mind was telling you that some financial number or external future circumstances would make you happy, safe, and comfortable, he knew that was false. If it looked like figuring out February today was a good idea, he knew that it wasn't.

Like solving a math problem with too many variables, even your best solution for February would be a complete guess. The way to February wasn't through the spreadsheet. But perhaps the way to feeling safe and comfortable about the future was?

"The future doesn't exist," the Coach said flatly, becoming an umpire in the game of life. "All we have is right now. Longing for the past or trying to predict the future is a recipe for suffering. The past is history, the future is a mystery, but here we are right now. What if we don't have to solve February in this specific moment? Ah. Check it out. We now have more mental horsepower, more bandwidth, and more possibility available to

us, here, right now. What if you don't have to plan next
Tuesday's lunch menu in this very instant? We could say,
'chicken salad,' and come back to it in 30 minutes, right?" The
Client saw that there was no pressing deadline. Except the one
in his imagination.

"Even if some future decision looks really important, let's
agree that we can set those objectives and goals aside for right
now. Would that be okay with you? Because any goal you want
to create always starts at the same place. It starts right now."

The Coach asked the Client to consider his goals for the
future, but bring them back into the present. Considering what
he wanted to see or be or achieve in February, what did that goal
look like right now?

"A goal brought into the present moment," the Coach said,
"is called a *value*."

"What we value, right now, will guide our actions. If we
value finding some good food, we will make it or search for it or
ask someone for it . . . you get the idea, the Coach shared. "So,
before you go and plan ahead, look at where you are right now."

"First, notice that you have everything you need. Right now,
at this moment, there is no pressure. The bank isn't calling you
about some overdue loan. You are okay. So, slow down. Why do
you think that it's important to notice these things?"

After considering the question, the Client replied, "Because
no one is really good under unnecessary pressure."

The Coach agreed. "In fact, in those high-pressure
situations, the key is to look beyond the pressure. Like a
field-goal kicker in the final minutes of a tie game: you can't
think about the score, or the fans, or what you did in practice
last week. You have to keep your eye on the ball. You have to
play the game. You have to put one foot in front of the other.
And put that foot on the ball! Focusing anywhere else will

take you out of the game. The path to victory," the Coach continued, "means playing the game."

The Client replied, "I'm just not sure what game I'm supposed to be playing right now."

The Coach saw exactly what he meant. Robbed of his routine, the Client was trying to create one. The certainty of his job – it certainly sucked and he hated it – was what he wanted to recreate. His work was gone. The gig was lost in the sands of time.

Luckily, the Coach understood that what was unknown was much greater than what was known. In fact, whatever the Client was going to do next was going to come from the unknown. That was how the future worked.

If the Coach had a superpower, it was his ability to enter into the unknown without discomfort or fear. And he helped his clients to do the same.

The Client knew that planning for the future from a place of worry, pressure, concern, or desperation wasn't going to make anything easier. Having everything you need made everything easier. That perspective wasn't a construct or a hypothetical. The Coach stepped him through some reminders of who he was, helping to ease his mind.

The Coach wasn't offering some clickbait strategy to get him to feel good about himself. The Coach wasn't telling him the prettiest lie he could think of and asking the Client to believe it. The Coach wasn't peddling some psychological juju designed to help him believe in some version of himself that didn't exist. The Coach was focused on finding truth. The truth that would set the Client free.

"But how am I going to be able to reach my goals?" the Client asked.

The Coach knew that there was a larger conversation on order. What, specifically, were those goals? he wondered to himself. How had his goals changed, given the shift in circumstances? And what did those goals – and goal-setting – really look like, for the Client?

The men set aside some time later in the week for a Zoom conversation. Before they hung up, the Coach asked the Client for a difficult commitment.

"Don't look at that spreadsheet until we talk again."

Whatever role or opportunity the Client would find, he would find it in the unknown. And that was exactly where they were headed.

CHAPTER 16.
CRUSHING
YOUR GOALS

When you
know better

you
do better.

MAY ANGELOU
AUTHOR AND POET

"I'm going to show you how to bend time," the Coach said.

He was seated in front of an impossibly perfect Zoom background that the Client later discovered was real. Somehow the Coach had managed to get a soft-focus camera for Zoom calls in his home office. Behind him were two white orchids, framing two abstract paintings suffused with orange, blue, and brown hues. The entire scene was built atop a mid-century-modern credenza, next to a silver-gray chair that appeared stolen from Don Draper's office. The overall effect was something you might see in a TV studio, if a network produced a show called "In the Coach's Office" and filmed it entirely in Zoom.

The Client began with timelines. Time was a concern for him: it always seemed to be running out.

The time it would take for his severance to expire. How much time he would need to sign and return the documents. How much time it might take to launch his business, he said, alluding to his future goals. "Because time is money," he told the Coach.

The Coach wanted to introduce a different perspective – one that didn't have a deadline attached. "What if there were many more knobs to turn and levers to pull, outside of these financial possibilities?" the Coach replied. The Client was stressed out. He wasn't going to fall for the Jedi mind trick.

"If you turn off the engine, the car won't take you anywhere," he replied. "What if I run out of gas? The money and the time are real concerns."

The Coach felt like those were not the Droids he was looking for. He asked the Client to set aside the financial concerns, for a moment. After all, didn't he have enough money right now, and for the immediate future? Yes, the Client admitted. Yes, he did. The Coach always wanted to focus on real problems, not imaginary ones. And from a peaceful state of mind, possibilities are more easily accessed. Time, the Coach knew, could become an ominous fire-breathing dragon in times of stress. He also knew that dragons weren't real.

"Worrying about some future event that's a potential scenario and may perhaps happen is like solving a hypothetical puzzle inside a fictional riddle. I know those financial concerns look real, and I'm not saying they're not. But let's set that timeline aside for a moment and I promise we will come back to it. Fair enough?"

The Client agreed. He spoke of his goals and what he knew about goal-setting. The Coach was curious: he suspected the Client had considered new options for his career, since he had already wanted to leave the company. The idea of entrepreneurship had shown up more than once.

The Coach surmised that the Client already had a goal in mind for his next step. What was it?

The Client responded quickly. "I want to launch my own consulting business. I need a BHAG to help me get there," he explained.

The Coach recognized the term: it stood for "Big Hairy Audacious Goal." The idea behind BHAG was a simple one. Having audacious or outrageous goals was a way to stretch yourself, to see what you were made of. Aim for the stars, the saying goes, and you just might land on the moon. Of course, there's no oxygen on the moon.

Every salesperson knows how new quotas are designed to stretch toward stratospheric goals. The Client wasn't in sales, but he had seen how goals were always set to drive greater performance. He believed he needed to define his own stretch goal in order to achieve . . . well, what exactly? In the absence of clear direction, that inner knowing was eluding him at the moment. So, the Client turned to what he had been told.

He tried to turn a four-letter-acronym into a lifestyle.

The BHAG acronym was a modern retelling of the Pygmalion effect. In a nutshell, the Pygmalion effect says that great expectations produce great results.

"What's a Pygmalion?" the Client asked. He wondered if it was a way to make bacon or something.

The Coach explained the details about the Greek myth of Pygmalion.

"Pygmalion was an ancient king who also happened to be a sculptor. He carved a statue out of stone, creating what he believed was the perfect woman, and he named the sculpture Galatea. Through the magic of the gods – this is Greek mythology, after all – the statue came to life. And Pygmalion fell in love with the statue."

The Client was confused. "So where exactly were the high expectations? Did Pygmalion expect that he could bring a statue to life and so the gods granted his wish or something? This story doesn't make sense."

"Actually, it makes a lot of sense," the Coach said, "when you consider that it's not the story of high expectations at all. It's the story of a king who fell in love with a false idol of his own creation."

The Coach explained that Pygmalion adored an artificial construct. He fooled himself, and became a fool in the process, not only by fooling himself into thinking he could shape the perfect woman but also by falling in love with a complete and utter fiction. His Big Hairy Audacious Goal was a complete fake, and he became smitten with a lie. "Does that sound like a good strategy to you?" he asked.

Social scientists borrowed the premise of high expectations leading to great results in a study they named the Pygmalion effect. The premise of the deeply debated study, released in 1968 by Robert Rosenthal and Lenore Jacobsen,[1] was that higher teacher expectations created greater student results. Like a self-fulfilling prophecy, low expectations, particularly around test results, would deliver low test performance. At least, that was the idea. While the book proved its premise, as most books often do, there was a little bit of a problem with the Pygmalion effect.

Specifically, it didn't work.

Scientists and scholars disputed the findings of the Pygmalion effect, which also came to be called the Rosenthal effect. Using high expectations to drive higher results was a premise that was difficult to replicate. Duplication wasn't difficult because of the research; the hypothesis just wasn't true. Not everyone conforms to desired results. Not everyone performs well under high expectations.

"Why do you think that is?" the Coach asked.

After a pause, the Client said, "No one is at their best with a gun to their head. Or when trying to live up to some false construct. Seems like high expectations can be discouraging. Or intimidating. Or those expectations remind you of who you are not."

"Exactly," the Coach replied. "When a goal reminds you of who you are not, that's the definition of discouragement. Creating some ideal, or having someone else tell you what that ideal outcome is, creates a Catch-22: who are you if you don't reach your goal? What if Galatea doesn't love you back? It's the opposite of what you need – what you really need – to pursue something. Reaching for some big hairy audacious anything is setting up an artificial construct," the Coach said. "Creating a reminder of what you don't have, or of who you aren't, and reminding yourself of your shortcomings and imperfections . . . well, how is that easier? Where's the encouragement and enrichment and excitement in all of that 'less-than' stuff?"

The Client considered the disconnect, pondering the fact that no one could create the perfect partner, from stone or flesh. The Pygmalion effect isn't about setting lofty goals, he realized. It's a story about people who fall in love with false creations. Impossible situations. He noticed how the researchers who tried to make the case for high expectations ended up with low results.

Just like the story of the king and his statue, the Pygmalion effect is pure myth. Not a strategy for success.

The Coach tried to bring it all home for the Client. "Have you ever created a construct, around artificial circumstances or expectations, and fallen in love with your own creation – only to be heartbroken when it doesn't love you back or give you the results you expect?"

The voice inside the Client's head screamed, "Could he be speaking of your job?" But the Client wasn't exactly convinced about where it was all headed, so he said, "What's wrong with wanting big goals for yourself?"

"Nothing," the Coach said quickly. "There's nothing wrong with wanting to make the most beautiful statue you can, for example. But here's where big goals can get you into big trouble: when your relationship to those goals doesn't make achievement easier."

He wondered out loud, "Why embrace a myth and try to build your life or your business around it? The stories only lead to disappointment and discouragement. What if Pygmalion had realized he was in love with a statue? Misinformed expectation does not lead to high results. How could that make anything easier?"

The Client looked past his monitor, at the desk in his office. A picture of his wife and two girls, taken outside the Teacup ride at Disneyland, sat on his desk. The smiles on their faces were the most real things he had ever seen. Their perfection wasn't manufactured or sculpted. Pure joy was a permanent fixture inside the wooden frame that held the image.

Beside the photo of his girls sat a picture of his team at a work retreat. In the middle of the 10 team members in the photo, the Client stood next to an easel, holding a paintbrush in one hand. On the easel was a canvas, and on the canvas was a painting of a bowl of fruit. The colors were vibrant, the shadows were perfectly captured. The painting was his. In his left hand, he held a wooden trophy. The square base of the trophy was made of a dark wood. A large empty wineglass was affixed to the wooden base. He had won first prize in the art contest, conducted at an offsite location where wine and painting combined to create memories. The most amazing thing about the picture? Before the evening started, he didn't even know he could paint.

Most of his pictures were digital, but these two framed mementos sat side by side. Love and resourcefulness stared back at him from inside wooden frames. Recalling the night of his artistic victory, and the wineglass trophy, he remembered how he had no expectations whatsoever of creating that work when the evening began. An engineer artist? Who could have imagined? He hadn't wanted or wished for some statue made out of wood and glass. He had no identity around being a painter – he just picked up the paintbrush and followed the guidance from the group leader. He shared what he saw as he picked out the colors and hues.

First prize was his. Even though that wasn't really the goal at all. In fact, when he had no goal in mind whatsoever, he realized, he actually tended to play his best. He discovered new skills. He found fun inside of an office function. He didn't know he couldn't paint, and so he did it. He didn't talk himself out of it, he just did it. And, for the picture on the left, there was absolutely no goal or expectation anywhere to be found. The expression on his wife's face told a wordless story of joy and connection. One common element in both pictures: everything inside those frames was effortless.

"What happens if you hold on loosely to your goals?" the Coach asked. "For example, you've said that your goal is to start your own business. But what if a company comes along and offers you a higher salary at a place where you would love to work? Do you reject the offer outright, because it doesn't align with your self-proclaimed BHAG? Please understand, there is nothing wrong with wanting to launch your own business. Or with taking another job. Or any choice you wish to make around your career. I'm here for all of it! But a goal gives direction and intention, not always a destination. If we hold on too tightly, we miss opportunities. We live life with blinders on, calling it 'focus' instead of keeping our eyes and ears open for possibility."

The Coach slid his chair out of frame, exiting stage right. He returned with a gray and white cat in his lap. The cat sat on the coach like a grateful pillow with ears and a tail. "Hold on loosely," the Coach said, petting the cat, "and notice possibilities. Because living with blinders on is never easier. You might miss the opportunity that's right in front of you, because it's not part of the mythical BHAG you created." The cat sat up and looked to his right. Meowing, the cat bounced off the Coach's lap and disappeared from the screen.

"Human beings are really good at making stuff up," the Coach said. "We create plans and projections and proclamations – stories inside our minds about perfect statues and how high expectations are a requirement for high performance. I'm not saying that having goals is completely useless. It's not. What I'm talking about is our relationship with our goals. We build up all these 'if/then' statements: 'if the boss doesn't go for this idea, then I'm a failure. If she doesn't love me back, I'm a loser. If this doesn't go exactly the way I've scripted and sculpted it out, I'm a disaster.' Hanging your identity on an outcome is a recipe for defeat. Because the expectation is based on a misunderstanding. Yet we do it all the time!"

The Client thought of the king who loved a statue. Had he built an entire museum around the statue as well? And, like that king, was he building expectations and identities around his mythical, unlaunched business idea? He needed to work with the way things are, not some imagined construct from inside his head. Having goals wasn't the problem – attaching to them was.

The Coach said, "There's something else that we do even better than wondering and wandering into the future, making up scenarios of what failure looks like, building some artificial Galatea into our lives. There's something much better than manufacturing pressure, or high expectations, or both. What human beings do really, really well – and by the way, when I say 'human beings' that means you and me – is *figure things out*. We figure things out when they come to us."

The Client looked again at the image of his artistic adventure. He recalled the unusual feel of the paintbrush in his hand. He remembered trying to Bob Ross a few things, using what looked like a spatula to insert shadows and colors. How had he done that? Well, he figured it out when it came to him. He didn't do it for the prize, or for any goal whatsoever. The picture on his desk, taken just after the paint had dried, reflected the surprise and celebration of a very satisfying result.

"We get things done," the Client said, bringing his attention back to the conversation and remembering how to win. "Not by grinding and figuring and striving and struggling, but by dealing with what comes to us, moment to moment. Like you do when you're surfing." *Or painting,* he thought to himself. *Or spending time with these two beautiful little girls at an amusement park, where every moment is new.*

What others might call goals or accomplishments he saw as the aftereffects of a life that was authentic. The result of putting one foot in front of the other. Or one color on the canvas at a time. Sometimes, he thought, not having a specific goal could be a path to really creating something amazing, natural, and easy. Because things get easier when you don't necessarily have a rigid, fixed goal in mind. Sometimes an intention is all it really takes, he realized.

The Coach nodded his head. "Taking life moment by moment, understanding that we are part of an infinite and benevolent universe, where we can and will figure things out as they present themselves, is . . . what's the word I'm looking for?"

The Client replied, "Easier?"

The Coach smiled in acknowledgment. "I don't know how surfing works, but this is how surfing works: we figure it out. This is how getting fired works: we figure it out. Some things are pleasant, some not so much, but we *figure it out.* Moment to moment we figure it out. Why set outrageous expectations, unless you want to create undue pressure or discouragement around your goals? Who does well under those conditions?"

"I just feel like," the Client said, "I should have this figured out by now."

He had been unemployed for exactly 74 hours.

He was free but he kept trying to reinsert himself into a new prison.

He had been told, and he had seen, that it wasn't all up to him. But that realization took place in Austin. When he still had a job. So now that truth looked different. Why?

The Coach said, "I think your timing is off. The problem with success is that we don't see it in the present tense," he said.

"I have a friend, an amazing coach by the name of Michael Neill. He wrote this book," the Coach said, bending down and leaving the frame to pick up a white paperback. He held it to the screen, and the Client saw the title: *Creating the Impossible*.[2]

"You should watch his TED talks, by the way. I'll send you the links; remind me later. Anyway, Michael Neill says that there is an inevitability of success over time."

The Coach continued with a cryptic remark. "Bending time might make you get better faster," he reasoned. "Here, let me share this article with you – can you see it on the screen?" The Client nodded, while the Coach clicked and picked a window for Zoom.

"Given enough time," the Coach continued, quoting from the *Forbes*[3] article as he highlighted the words with his mouse, "we can figure out all kinds of things: from the path to the C-suite to career changes and more. Instead of recognizing that success takes time, we cling to ideas like 'overnight success' and put our own thinking around timelines – and that thinking focuses on an artificial construct that keeps us from being truly successful.

"Here, look at this," the Coach said. He scrolled down and this is what the Client read:

Most people define success based on where they aren't, instead of where they are. Have you ever found yourself saying something like this?

- If I were successful, I'd be a vice president *by now*.
- I should have 10,000 Instagram followers *by now*.
- *By now* I should have my own business and start making mailbox money, then I would be successful.
- I should be married *by now*, I should own a six-bedroom house with a pool *by now*, my Tesla should have arrived *by now*, etc.

What happens if we stop "shoulding" ourselves, and eliminate the words "by now"? If we're going to find true success, those two words have to go.

Michael breaks it down like this. "I can see that the enemies of success are pressure and discouragement, because pressure kills creativity, stifles performance, creates tension. And discouragement is just hopelessness, which leads to resistance and giving up. So now we have to find ways to motivate ourselves and overcome reluctance and all that garbage, to get past the barrier of by now." Michael doesn't suggest that eliminating deadlines and pressure is the answer: instead, he says that our relationship with deadlines, obligations, and "future success" needs to change.

What would happen if you redefined success in the present? Or do you prefer some pressure-packed, discouragement-filled vision of the future, based on what you lack and built on a made-up timeline? Michael says, "We're focused on success in terms of the future." And often: focused on what it is we can't do, or don't have, or what outcome should be here by now.

The Coach stopped the screen share. "What do you make of all that?" he asked the Client.

"I really get the idea of dropping the 'by now,'" he said. "It definitely makes things easier. But actually, that is easier said than done. Because we always put timelines on things. I mean, there's a monthly budget, and the amount of cash that you have on hand. If you don't make more money, you will run out of cash in a fixed amount of time. So you better have some new ideas. And some new numbers in your bank account – by now!"

The Coach smiled, because he had often felt the same way. Time was a very real and important construct to him, once upon a time. He had changed his relationship with time, however. Now he could bend time to his needs. He still made it to his appointments and got up with his alarm clock. But the clock served him, not the other way around. Time was not his master, *by now*. Time never would be. Success was all around him. Not tied to a deadline or aligned with his calendar.

"How long," the Coach asked, "did you date your wife before you got married?"

"Eleven months," the Client said. "How about you?"

"Five years," the Coach said. "So who got it right? Both, and neither – because what was right for you wasn't right for me, and vice versa. Have you ever noticed that you don't really 'win' at marriage? It's always a shared victory. Same with the amount of time it takes to start a life together. If someone asked how long it takes to date someone before you get married, well, you and I are living proof that 'actual mileage may vary.' Doesn't make one marriage better or worse than the other, does it?"

"So often, we fool ourselves into thinking that we have the 'Stopwatch of Success': in other words, we know how long it takes to achieve success. I mean, even how long it takes to boil an egg can change when you are in Denver instead of Des Moines, because of the altitude! A soccer game is always ninety minutes, except when it's not. Except when penalties make it longer. How much longer? Nobody knows, until you play the game! So, success can be a moving target. Why do we think we know how long a thing is going to take, like finding the perfect person, or landing a great job, or starting a business, when we absolutely do not?"

"Because we want things to be here by now," the Client said, simply.

"And what's wrong with that?" the Coach asked. Answering his own question, he said, "Absolutely nothing! We want things, that's totally normal, and we get the timing wrong all the time. Also totally normal! Remember what Michael Neill said," the Coach continued, "we've got to stop 'shoulding' ourselves. What would happen if we did?"

As the Client considered the possibilities, the Coach went on, "Things get easier when you stop looking at where you should be – and start with where you are. Wasting time on where you should be is a great way to get smashed by a wave that you didn't see coming – or miss the one you really need. Getting clear on where you are is the only positioning that matters. Because, as I've said before, the future always comes from the same place: right now."

He put the *Forbes* article back on the screen, and he read the words silently, along with the Client:

> Is it possible to be out of work, and still be successful? Can you be unmarried, unemployed, invisible on Instagram, fill in the blank with some other label, and still be successful? The answer is yes. Where you are is not who you are. You are more than your circumstances. And success isn't some future outcome, based on a job title, dollar figure,
>
> *(continued)*

(continued)

relationship status, or clever filter on social media. Success is available to you, right now. Drop your definition of where you should be. Worrying about where you should be is a perfect recipe to miss where you are. The challenge is: we don't like where we are right now.

When the Client read that last sentence, all he said was, "I can relate to that."

"What if," the Coach said, "there are no mistakes?"

The Client blinked at the screen. "What?"

"What happened this week wasn't a mistake. Your wife said it was a gift!"

The Client remembered the conversation. He flashed on how hard it was to get started, then how much easier it was once he did. What he predicted – an imminent, irrefutable catastrophe – was the exact opposite of what unfolded. The broken blue dish sat inside the dustpan. Shattered pieces, caught and held. The Client remembered the kindness in his wife's eyes, and the touch of her hands on his face before she kissed him. The memory was a gift – and it all felt easier.

"Was she wrong?" the Coach asked. "When I think back about the 'mistakes' in my life, I see that I was just doing the best I could with the thinking I had at the time. Some of my greatest 'mistakes' have put me on the path that I'm on today. So many things that I once called 'mistakes,' I now see that they have shaped me in a way that brings gratitude. Not shame. Not blame. They help me play the game."

"You know that phrase by Maya Angelou, 'When you know better, you do better'? Isn't that true? What I once called a mistake I now see as grace – because it made me who I am. My choices, especially the ones I would never make again, have given me a new perspective. What some call mistakes I call a gift. Or, when I'm really at my best, I don't waste time with labels at all."

"What are 'mistakes' anyway? They are the way I learned to walk and the way you learned to surf. Once upon a time I couldn't ride a bike or drive a car. Was all of that a mistake, or a failure of some kind? No, it was just part of my development. Oh man, I'm grateful for it all!"

"Take a look at this last section," the Coach said.

So we make choices and decisions based on a mindset of what should be here, by now. Unfortunately, that's not how success really works. Putting a made-up timeline on how long things should take is a recipe for suffering, disillusionment, and disappointment. Especially when the timing on everything – from kick-starting the economy to restarting your career – is in flux.

Arthur Ashe famously said, "Start where you are. Do what you can. Never give up." Success starts in this moment, whenever you are ready to see it. Even in the midst of undesired circumstances there are still choices to make. Actions to take. Reasons to stay awake.

But hopefully you've realized that *by now*.

"Wow," the Client said.

The Coach wanted to make sure that the Client internalized these ideas around success, and timing, and more. "Write out what you've discovered today," he said to the Client. "Focus on what you heard that made things easier. And, before I let you go, I want to give you another homework assignment. Would you be up for that?"

The Client eagerly agreed.

"First, write out your values," the Coach said. "What is it that really matters to you, right now?"

The Coach pointed him to a book by Karen Mangia called *Success from Anywhere*.[4] "Check out Chapter 3, 'The Stress-Free Experiment,'" he said. "Once you have your values – things like family, personal development, service, openness, or whatever the case may be for you – then write out how you see those values demonstrated in your everyday life."

This exercise, the Coach explained, has been shown in numerous scientific studies to produce powerful and proven results around greater resilience, improved relationships, reduction of stress, and even improved physical health.

Reading from the book, the Coach shared the following passage:

How do your values come into play, in the midst of difficulty, challenge, or conflict?

Remember, your values are unique to you. There is no value judgment on your values!

The choices you make must be your own. Otherwise, you'll end up conducting a stress-free experiment on behalf of your parents, your boss, or your ex-boyfriend. Let them do the work on their own!

In the middle of stress, go to your values. When confronted with uncertainty and change, go to your values. Getting defensive? Go to your values. And know that your

(continued)

(continued)

values are simply an expression of preference, in a given moment (which is why it's useful to look at your values, and journal how you see your values showing up, on a daily basis).

"Spend at least 10 minutes a day writing out how you see your values coming to life, in the actions you take every day. Do it every day. Or don't. Do it when it's right for you. This isn't an obligation, it's an exploration. You will know how often you need to do this exercise. But try it. Try out the 'Stress Free Experiment.' And see how your goals look, right here and right now.

"Sometimes the discipline we need isn't found in pure willpower or grit. Willpower goes out from time to time. Just like the power grid in Texas." Both of the men laughed, and then they stopped and looked at each other with raised eyebrows. They shared a look that said, "How the hell did that happen?" and, simultaneously, "Thank god that's over!"

The Coach went back to the idea of values, saying, "The point is: discipline isn't based on willpower. Discipline is simply remembering what you want. Write down your values. Do you still have that notebook I gave you?"

He did. He held it up in front of his camera.

"Keep that notebook close by to jot down your thoughts."

"Why?" the Client said. "Is there something else I need to write down?"

"Yes," the Coach said. "Keep going on your list. Call me when you've discovered sixty ways to make things easier."

"Why don't you just tell me what they are?" the Client asked.

"Whose journey are you on?" the Coach replied. The Client had to experience his own point of view. The Client had to take the ride. "Let me ask you: is life easier?"

The Client nodded as he looked down at his desk. His planning for the future had gotten easier. His relationship with time had gotten easier. His relationship with his wife and his daughters had also gotten easier. He was home.

Literally, yes, he was home. But personally, spiritually, and professionally: he was *home*.

"Almost everything," the Coach had told him, "can be made easier." The Client was starting to experience what he meant.

He still wondered about having big goals, though. He liked the idea of putting goals in an obvious place, where he could see them and remember what it was that he wanted. Like discipline, which might just be one of his values. He looked at his desk once again and saw the picture of his family. Maybe he had his goals in plain sight after all.

But right now, he needed to know how to launch his own consulting business.

Notes

1. Schaedig, Derek, "Self-Fulfilling Prophecy and the Pygmalion Effect," August 24, 2020, *Simply Psychology,* https://www.simplypsychology.org/self-fulfilling-prophecy.html
2. Neill, Michael, *Creating the Impossible: A 90-day Program to Get Your Dreams Out of Your Head and into the World* (Hay House, 2018).
3. Westfall, Chris, "From Your Career to Coronavirus: Drop These 2 Words to Find Success," *Forbes,* July 6, 2020, https://www.forbes.com/sites/chriswestfall/2020/07/06/career-coronavirus-2-words-to-find-success-leadership/
4. Mangia, Karen, *Success from Anywhere* (John Wiley & Sons, 2021).

CHAPTER 17.
CREATING THE FUTURE

What people think of as the moment of discovery

is really the discovery of the question.

JONAS SALK
INVENTOR OF THE POLIO VACCINE

There are a million ways to surf.

As long as you're smiling, you're doing it right.

UNKOWN

The Client noticed the high arches of freeway above and around the MoPac Expressway. In the past, a highway was just a way to get somewhere. But on his drive around North Austin, he noticed the differences between where he had been and where he was going. Heading into the residential area, restaurants and retail shops piqued his curiosity. He noticed that there was a lot of activity on the sidewalks of Austin on this fine midwinter morning. A cool breeze made its way into the SUV.

With his left elbow sticking out of the window, the Client considered how things had changed for him. He had the impulse to explore other job opportunities, but ultimately realized that he valued something other than the stability of the consistent paycheck. Entrepreneurship was his intended destination, and he was hoping to find new ideas to help launch his business. His Coach had encouraged him to explore the unknown. He didn't need a GPS to help him get there.

The Client had begun socializing the idea of starting a consulting business, designed around "M&A activity" (in other words, mergers and acquisitions – buying businesses or acquiring technology that could help expand a company's product portfolio, or their distribution network, or perhaps rounding out their capabilities in other ways). He wasn't exactly sure of the form, but he was clear in the intention. He wanted to become a broker for new ideas and new ventures.

The initiative was a rebranding of his previous work experience, which seemed like the kind of reframing of his goals that aligned with his present values.

"Do the doable," his Coach had told him. "That's how you create the impossible. You don't need anything hairy or audacious. Just do the doable, and you will move forward, with ease and encouragement, putting one foot in front of the other."

His next opportunity, the Coach had shared, would probably be one step to the right or left of where he was now. "Don't search for it," the Coach had said.

"Searching implies that something is missing. It's not. You have skills and talents to offer; they are not missing," he shared. "Notice where you might like to offer those gifts."

Easing past the lawns and landscaping of the Coach's neighborhood, the Client reflected on their first conversation. The familiar setting reminded the Client of who he could be.

Today, he wanted to explore new insights into accelerating his consulting business. The Coach met him at the door and greeted him with open arms.

The men returned to the outdoor patio. The space was the same. One of the men was not.

"Tell me how to really launch a consulting business," the changed man said.

"Is your business a product business, or a service business?" the Coach replied. He liked to start upstream.

"My business is based on service," the Client responded. "Consulting services to help companies acquire new technology or even acquire other companies. To help fill gaps in their capabilities. I want to know exactly how to leverage LinkedIn, and maybe Facebook advertising, to contact new prospects. And then, once I've created my lead magnet, or funnel, I want to know how to turn names into numbers and hit my million-dollar goals. Do I need a whitepaper, or a video, or maybe even a book before I really get going?"

The Coach chuckled to himself. Old habits die hard.

We have everything we need inside of us, he knew, but we always look outside for the tools and fixes first. Lots of Internet millionaires had made fortunes peddling those lead magnets, and he didn't deny their success.

He knew that those funnels, fixes, and Facebook strategies only make sense when they come from the inside out. Like going on a hike: when it shows up on the journey that you need a drink of water, you reach for the water bottle. Not before, and not after. And not when somebody else tells you to drink. If it makes sense to buy $10,000 worth of Facebook ads, you will know it when you see it – not because somebody else told you to do it.

The sky was gray and filled with clouds. There was a slight chill in the air, and a breeze made its way into the patio as the men spoke.

"When we realize how resourceful we are," the Coach shared with the Client, "new resources show up. Here's where to start finding your own resources. Because I don't know if LinkedIn or Facebook or a whitepaper is what you need, and maybe you're wondering the same thing," he said. "I wonder . . . if you don't know what resources you need, what happens if you start by *being* a resource?"

The Coach was pouring the tea into the glasses once again.

"A resource?" the Client asked. "What kind of a resource?"

The Coach said, "I don't know." And he took a long drink of tea.

The Coach looked out at the trees, to make sure no new leaves had fallen to the ground. He noticed the clouds in the sky. He looked at the building cranes in the distant skyline.

He cocked his brown suede boot and looked at it. Nope, nothing was stuck to it. What a beautiful day.

The Client looked over at the Coach.

He knew the Coach had built lead magnets, video programs, courses, best-selling books, whitepapers, and more. Why wasn't he doing more to fix what was broken?

The Coach shattered the silence. "Who can *you* help the most?" he asked.

"Who, besides yourself, can you really, really serve? I'm asking you professionally right now – who can you help the most? And who can you help in a way that would make you say, '*Yes!* That is awesome, I love doing that and serving people in that way.' Because your business is service, right?"

"Right" the Client replied.

"Then serve. Serve people. Be a resource." He leaned back and siphoned off some more tea.

"When I was starting my career as a speaker," the Coach said, "I went to a brilliant coach in Dallas. I told him I wanted to be a professional speaker. I'd done lots of speaking in my corporate career. I wanted to branch out on my own. I knew this guy, this coach, he was a Hall of Fame speaker. I thought for sure he had the recipe. I said, 'Can you help launch my career'?"

"Sounds kinda familiar," the Client said, trying the tea himself. "What did he say?"

"Speak."

"What do you mean, 'Speak'? I don't understand," the Client said.

"'Speak anytime. Anywhere. Any fee. Any audience.' That was what he told me. And from him to me to you, I'm telling you the same thing. Your business is different, you're not trying to be a speaker, I get that. But you are trying to provide a service. So, serve."

The Client leaned back in his chair. He considered what being a resource meant – and what kind of resource he could be.

"Serve deeply. Serve people in a way that they cannot serve themselves. Serve people so that they say, 'Wow. This guy!'" the Coach was pointing at him. "Serve generously, and graciously. Serve at the deepest level you possibly can. Consider what that might mean to you. What that might mean to your potential clients. Right now, without any clients, that service means being a resource."

"Let me share with you a truth that, to me, looks undeniable. The truth I see is this: all around us are people who need help with something." A flock of birds shot into view, darting over the roofs and rolling hills outside of the patio. The Client followed their movements. The intricate relationship between the birds created a V in the sky. He saw a flock of birds, but he was observing *connection*. His eyes brought in the image but his mind processed something more than just wings and shapes. The interdependence in a flock of birds wasn't a goal or an expectation. Association was a part of nature. The birds didn't have to go it alone. Together, their journey continued, into the blue sky. Together, a group of individual birds moved as one, shifting into a modified arrow, always pointing toward their destination. A destination they would discover together.

The Coach watched the birds as well, considering how all creatures need each other. "Nothing of any value happens without the help of other people," he said. The Client looked at him and smiled. The men sat silently for a moment. Then the Coach spoke again, as he shifted his weight in the chair. "When I go to a restaurant, the waiters and the cooks and the bartender all work together to create an amazing service, an amazing meal, an amazing memory. Especially at a top-flight restaurant. The restaurant model is a great place to learn about great service.

So what is the service you would love to create?" he asked rhetorically.

"Think of your business like a waiter in a white-tablecloth restaurant. That waiter is a resource for the table – for all the guests at the table, right? That waiter is an expert on the menu. That waiter might even be able to get you some things that aren't on the menu. Maybe even get you a seat at the chef's table back in the kitchen, if you know what you're doing. Am I right?"

The Client knew that he was.

"What does the server at a top-tier restaurant do? First, she's gonna ask you if you have any allergies. Why? So that she won't bring you the pecan-encrusted flounder if you've got a nut allergy. In fact, if you ask for a dish that conflicts with your allergy, she won't bring it. That's not denial of service. Sometimes refusing to do something is service at the highest possible level. Sometimes saying no is the most helpful thing you can say. Because that's a service that helps people get out of their own way. Service that keeps people safe. Do you follow me?" the Coach asked.

Seeing the Client nod, he continued, "Whatever you order is gonna be A-OK with the server. She knows the menu backward and forward, and if you tell her what you like she will make sure you get it. She wants you to be happy, healthy, and satisfied. She knows about wine and she knows how to find a pairing that might be unexpectedly delicious. Even if you are a fabulous connoisseur of great wine, that server has a perspective worth listening to. Because she knows the menu. She knows what wines go best with the food. That's her job.

"Her job is to create an experience for you," the Coach said, leaning in on the word *experience*. "So that you never want to eat anywhere else. That unforgettable experience, in my mind, is world-class service. And that server is a resource that deserves whatever tip you give her. Do you see that?

"Service," the Coach went on, "creates experiences. Experiences create exchange. Be a resource that provides service, in your own way. And be that resource for any audience. Any time. Anywhere. Everywhere you go, there are eight billion people on this planet. They all need help with something. I can't fix somebody's plumbing or heal a sick Chihuahua. Those are not my gifts. Or yours. Your service is unique. Your service is based on your gifts. Your values. Your skills. Your talents. You start your business because you want to serve. So start serving."

The Coach lifted the silver pitcher and poured tea into both glasses.

"Who do you know, right now, who's struggling with an area of their business where you could help them? And if the answer is, 'I'm not sure,' I like your style. Because, when you think about it, 'I'm not sure' is exactly where your next paycheck is right now. If you're wondering where the money for next year is going to come from, it's going to come from wherever it is right now. And how much of that money shows up will be in proportion to the service – the resource – that you provide.

"Help somebody. Let me say it again: Help somebody. Serve. Create exchange, by exchanging your ideas as a resource for someone who needs your help. In some way, go make life easier for someone else. Serve in the best way you know how. And for anyone who crosses your path, make a simple commitment."

"What commitment is that?" the Client asked.

The Coach asked a question before he offered an answer. "Can you agree that 'service' is one of your values? And that you want to see service demonstrated in your everyday life?"

The Client already had "service" as an important value. He had journaled about it in the notebook, and he was eager to share what he had written with the Coach. He had even discovered more than 60 ways to make things easier. But, for now, he wanted to know where the Coach was headed. Because, inside of the Client, a feeling that some might call "instinct" or even "inner-knowing" was telling him that service was the key to everything he wanted for his business. He just needed to know how to capitalize on that impulse and turn his gut-feel into a scalable and healthy business.

"I love what you're saying about service," the Client said, "that idea is really resonating with me. I'm thinking about that high-end waiter, the server in the restaurant. Do you have any tips on how to turn service into revenues? I mean, how do I price my services? Do I go hourly, or what exactly?"

The Coach shook his head. "Hourly rates will cheat your client, even though they don't realize it," he said, "and hourly rates will always mean you are leaving money on the table. Consider that you might be the kind of coach or consultant who can solve issues very quickly, and perhaps even create substantial results in less than an hour. So an hourly contract is a disincentive. The hourly rate points you toward going slow, because the more hours you work, the more you make. You want to maximize your earnings, of course. But what looks like a 'good hourly rate' actually cheats the client, because they force you to go slow. They create an incentive for you to do only what is asked so that extending the timeline for results becomes the goal, which isn't a goal that works for anybody.

"If you are offering a service that can be shopped and bid – like video editing, or blog writing – then hourly makes sense because you are entering your services into a preexisting market. You have to charge at or near what the market will bear, if you want to get any work. That's true with consulting, to a certain extent, but there is a lot more flexibility based on the value you create. Even if you can create that value in minutes instead of hours. What I'm saying is that the value is what matters, not how long it takes you to create that value. And guess who determines that value?"

"The client?" the Client said.

"And the consultant or coach," he replied.

"When you consider your consulting services, you are creating a bespoke and tailored solution. Yes, that service can perhaps be found elsewhere. But never quite exactly the same as what you will provide. Therefore, charging by the hour will undercut your potential earnings – and I'll show you what I mean in a second." The Coach got up out of his chair and went into the house. Thirty-three seconds later, he emerged carrying a small whiteboard, three markers, and a felt eraser.

On the whiteboard, he wrote the word OUTCOMES on the right and HOURS on the left. "When I go into a company or a conference to deliver a keynote, I'm onstage for one hour. The fees for my keynotes make my hourly rate absolutely outrageous. Many people who charge by the hour, or pay by the hour, find what I earn to be an eye-popping sum considering the amount of time I'm standing on stage."

"But what people don't realize is the thousands of hours it's taken me to be able to stand on that stage. To share my insights. To craft my delivery and create my impact. Lots of folks don't understand the amount of time I've spent working with speakers' bureaus – they are like agents for professional speakers. Or talking with the client beforehand, or conducting interviews with people attending the conference. There's a lot of time involved before you step on stage."

"But still, the fee is never about me. Not my time. Not my experience. The experience that matters is the experience of the audience," the Coach explained.

"Let's say that I do a keynote in front of four hundred people. The message helps four salespeople – just four! – to close five million dollars in new business next year. Or maybe it helps the leadership team to reduce turnover among new employees by fifteen percent, saving the company millions of dollars. The end result is improved morale and employee engagement. What's that outcome worth? Well, you can decide for yourself, but the ROI on the conversation is at least a hundred times. A hundred times. Think about that. It's not the hours that matter. It's the outcome."

The Client considered the business model. He liked it.

"So how exactly do I charge?" he asked the Coach.

"What are you going to have for lunch next Tuesday?" the Coach responded. The Client remembered the lunch question.

The Coach went on. "Look, here's what I know about you, and you do too: when a client with a problem shows up, you will know. When you serve them, and you see that you can serve them more deeply, I know you will figure it out," he said "Just like lunch next Tuesday."

"Here's a question that I ask that always helps me. I start off with a couple of questions. First, can I help this person (or this company)? Second, do I want to? Because there are a lot of people I could help. But one of the perks of being an entrepreneur is that I get to choose my clients. Just as they choose me."

"Cheers," the Client said, raising his glass while the Coach did the same.

"Then, here's the big kahuna. The question that you want to notice, not look for, not search for, but notice when it shows up in the conversation. Because service always starts with a conversation, right? Here's the question: 'Do you want some help with that'?

"Do you want some help with that?" the Client repeated. "So you're asking someone if they want some help with something. Something that you've identified where you can be of service, in an area where you want to help them, right?"

Service, for the Client, centered on new business acquisitions. New technology. New sources of revenue. He wondered if he could help people to find and acquire companies. What might happen if he reached out to his network and his contacts, discovered those who wanted to sell their businesses, or their solutions, and asked a simple question? One question, around "wanting some help with that" – what could be easier?

"It's deceptively simple," the Coach interjected. "Business often is. So that's your homework assignment this time. Commit to have a conversation where naturally and authentically you ask someone if they want some help with something. Something that they value. Something that could result in some sort of outcome that would have a dollar figure attached to it, perhaps. Or some sort of need that, when it's fulfilled, people would pay you for that service. I can't say what they would pay you, exactly, but I can tell you this: your intuition will guide you when the moment appears. Your mission, should you choose to accept it, is to find someone you might be able to help and serve. And ask if they want some help with something. Commit to service. That's all."

"But first, have conversations. What could be easier than that? Conversations can start online. Or if you can go old-school and get somebody to pick up the phone, even better. Before you build a CRM system and start automating your emails, do the doable. Have conversations. Coffee shop convos, Zoom calls, whatever. The conversation is where it begins. If you are on social media, like LinkedIn or Twitter, go on there. But go there to be a resource."

"Comment on blogs in a way that's positive. Share content that isn't self-serving or a restatement of your résumé. Find ways to help people. And find ways to create the space that you need to discover what your resourcefulness really is. That space is what I call 'a conversation.' Whether you tweet it or tell it, a conversation is what you need. The conversation is still the most powerful tool in business, and I think it always will be."

"Inside that conversation, serve. Serve deeply and powerfully. Offer what you can to help the person right in front of you. Give your ideas. Do so freely and with generosity. Help without hesitation. 'You will have a hundred great ideas today,' a consultant once told me when I was first starting out, 'and you'll have another hundred tomorrow.' Creativity is infinite. You'll never run out of ideas. That's not how thought works. You can never run out of ideas. Don't be precious about your intellectual property or any of that nonsense. Share and serve. And look for an opportunity to say these seven words: 'Do you want some help with that?' If somebody says yes, then you've got a decision to make," the Coach said with a smile.

"What decision is that?" the Client asked.

"Just take the first step. Start a conversation. Ask the first question. The next one will reveal itself. Just like the answers will. And if it looks like you don't know where to turn, you're actually on the right track. Just remember who you are, stay in the game, stay curious. Your inner knowing – your instinct – is on its way."

"And if you are wondering how to get massive numbers of clients, and which email platform is best, and how to really leverage Instagram, let me ask you a different kind of question. How many clients do you need to launch your business? I'll make it multiple choice. A is seventy-two million, B is twenty-one, C is nine, and D is one."

"I'm going to go with D," the Client said.

"Good choice," the Coach offered. "All it takes is one. You aren't looking for every wave in the sea. You just need one.

"When someone says they would like some help with something, look in the direction of outcomes, not hours. What might that outcome be worth to them? What would it look like if the thing that was missing showed up in their life? In their business?"

For the Client, this business model was the exact way his conversation had started with the Coach. The Coach had provided him with a soft place to land, he realized. A space to be heard. The coaching conversations were a sandbox. A sandbox of service, where they could experiment. He could try out new ideas and experience new ways of looking at his life and his business.

The Coach wasn't another manager, holding him accountable for things he didn't want to do. In fact, their relationship was exactly the opposite. Inside of the Client, his relationship with obligations had changed. He still had things that he needed to do, but he did them with grace instead of grit – and it wasn't just because he was working from home. He'd done that dance before, during Covid. That choreography felt a lot more difficult when he was in his previous job.

He wasn't sure if his productivity was going up. But his stress was going down. He felt like he was living life more fully. Living his values. He still had a mortgage to pay, and the lease on the car, school tuition, and everything else. But he saw his finances differently now.

While it was true that he wasn't sure how he was going to launch his business or how it would do or even if he was cut out for entrepreneurship, none of those questions mattered right now. Come what may, he was okay. In this moment. Right now.

He could lose it all. Make a fortune. God knows what. But he was not in the business of trying to know the mind of God. Or trying to predict the future.

"What would you do," his Coach asked, "if you knew you had everything you need?"

From somewhere in the neighborhood, an unseen lawnmower started. The sound of the engine wasn't loud or distracting, just a steady hum. On the coffee table that separated the two men, a small cactus plant – no bigger than a deck of playing cards – was sitting inside a tiny white pot. Small white blooms dotted the head of the cactus. The men couldn't see it, but the cactus was growing. The cactus was whole and complete and had everything it needed inside of that little white pot. Human nature, the Client surmised, was part of nature. Growth wasn't always obvious, or within your field of vision, but it was always happening, nevertheless. The Client was much more than a cactus, but he was no less complete or whole. He couldn't see the yard being mowed, he couldn't see the grass growing, but he understood that completeness was all around him. Was it within him as well?

The Client knew, and it wasn't a question of belief, that he had everything he needed. He was resourceful and adaptable and creative and innovative and courageous, in this moment, right now. He saw those characteristics as a part of himself – much the same way that he saw the four fingers and a thumb on his left hand.

True nature was apparent to him. And human nature was who he was. It was "both, and."

He came to understand, at an instinctual level, that he was a spiritual being having a human experience. Meanwhile, he was also a human being having a spiritual experience. That wasn't some pile of Zen woo-woo; it was the way things worked. And who he was.

His was not a fictional identity of his own creation. Not anymore. The identity he possessed was his place in the universe, a universe that had his back.

The universe had brought him back. Back to his wife. Back from his horrible job. Back from his old frustrations and, yes, back to some new ones. Some frustrations even showed up back-to-back. Life was messy, not clean and tidy. And he was here for all of it. Good, bad, or indifferent, he wanted to play a new game.

His newfound identity wasn't without its challenges and uncertainties. But the way he faced those uncertainties wasn't with fear or foreboding. He had found another "f" word for the future he couldn't see.

Fun.

The universe had given him the chance to explore new ideas between Dallas and Austin and anywhere else creativity might take him. His instincts were stronger, he felt. Or maybe he just trusted them more?

No offense to Billy Joel, but it really wasn't a matter of trust. He was listening to himself more. Or was it even himself – who was doing the listening? Whoa. That idea was new.

Where did these new ideas and this new identity come from, he wondered? The same place that makes the acorns turn into oak trees, he guessed. Source? Universal mind? God? He didn't want to go further and try to explain it. Because he didn't need to. He didn't need to figure everything out. That wasn't his job. It wasn't up to him.

He didn't need to find a reason or craft an explanation. Instead, he saw life as a game. And he wanted to play full-out. Why not?

He recalled a quote from *Hamlet* that the Coach had shared with him: "There are more things in heaven and earth, Horatio, than are dreamt of in your philosophy." How true. The universe was bigger, broader, and fuller of possibility than his mind could calculate. That fact didn't make him feel insignificant, incomplete, or stupid; it energized him. He was a part of this ever-expanding universe, and it had his back.

The Client looked out at the trees. The gray clouds were breaking up, and sunlight was reentering pockets of sky. In the distance, a single hawk circled above the tailored backyards of the neighborhood, as the lawnmower continued to hum.

"Let me show you what I've got in my notebook," the Client said to the Coach.

CHAPTER 18.
UNDER THE BLUE SKY

Freedom is not worth having

if it doesn't include

the freedom to make mistakes.

MAHATMA GANDHI
CIVIL RIGHTS ADVOCATE FOR NON-VIOLENT CHANGE

"Sometimes freedom is right under your nose, and you don't even realize it," the Client said. The idea of "no mistakes" was giving him a sense of freedom that was opening up the conversation, he thought. "Thank you," he told the Coach.

He shared the notepad, where he had written down what he had discovered.

31. There is always hope. Find it. Hope makes things easier.

32. Zoom out. Zoom out some more. Go upstream.

33. Don't make the impersonal personal.

34. You are "both, and" – a spiritual being and human being. Don't deny either one, if you want to make things easier.

35. What if there are no mistakes?

36. Release resentment. The universe is neutral. Can you be neutral too?

37. When in doubt, wait it out. New thoughts are on their way.

38. What would you do if you knew you were safe and comfortable? (You are enough).

39. Slow down.

(continued)

(continued)

40. When tomorrow gets here, you will figure it out. Don't forget who you are!

41. Feeling safe, or feeling anything, is a state of mind. Not circumstances.

42. A goal brought into the present moment is called a value. Bring your future goals into the present moment. Why wait?

43. Write out how you see your values demonstrated, every day, in your life. Live your values.

44. What is unknown is much greater than the known. Discovery is where the fun is.

45. Planning from a place of pressure, worry, concern, or desperation doesn't make anything easier.

46. The truth will set you free. Because understanding what's true makes everything easier.

47. You don't need anything hairy and audacious to reach your goals. There's no oxygen on the moon.

48. Do the doable. It's the first step in creating the impossible.

49. Don't build up a myth and fall in love with your creation. See #47.

50. Human beings are great at making stuff up. And solving real problems. Both are easy, but only one is effective.

51. Moment to moment, we figure it out. Come back to the now, and it all gets easier.

52. *Success is always available. When we eliminate two words, success gets closer (those two words: by now).*

53. *We do not have the Stopwatch of Success. Bending time starts when we realize how often we get the timing wrong. And that there's nothing wrong with that!*

54. *Stop "shoulding" yourself. Nothing is easier in a woulda-coulda-shoulda world.*

55. *Where you are is not who you are. Don't overidentify with your circumstances.*

56. *What you once called a mistake can now be called grace. Or don't even label it at all. That's easier.*

57. *"Start where you are. Do what you can. Never give up." – Arthur Ashe*

58. *Discipline made easier: discipline is just remembering what you really want.*

59. *Be a resource. A generous resource that provides exceptional service. It makes it easier for others to see your value.*

60. *Life is service. Serve deeply, generously, and graciously.*

"And I found one more," the Client said. "I might just put this one at the top of the list."

"What is it?" the Coach asked.

"You don't have to figure it all out."

EPILOGUE

We must accept
finite disappointment.

but never lose
infinite hope.

MARTIN LUTHER KING, JR.
CIVIL RIGHTS ADVOCATE

Nine months later, the Client sent an email to the Coach.

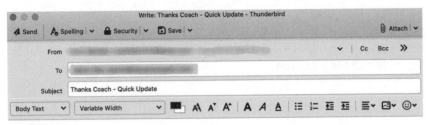

Hey there,

It's been a while! Hope this message finds you well!

My consulting business is going great. I've got three clients right now and I'm making twice as much as I did when I was at my job! WOW. I'm helping these companies to find innovative investment targets. My biggest client is in the process of buying a distributor that I brought to their attention. My previous employer didn't want to do the deal, but here we are! AWESOME

I didn't have to stalk people on LinkedIn, or spend a small fortune on Facebook ads. Like you said, business happens one conversation at a time. I reached out to my network. I reconnected with old friends. I became a new kind of resource, I guess. In the middle of conversations, I would find myself asking, "Do you want some help with that?" and you can guess the rest. The wave always comes to me. The pricing just kinda materialized – we figured it out together. The first two clients I had, I priced things too low and worked a lot of hours for not a lot of money. But hey, live and learn ~ LOL

My relationship with my wife and kids is spectacular. I've never felt closer to them. Especially my girls. I know we weren't necessarily working on relationships but that's been a side effect of our time together. My relationship with time and deadlines changed. My relationship with work changed completely. The fact that my personal relationships deepened…well, all I can say is: thank you for pointing me toward my values. The journey goes on! Hope you are having a good one.

I'm grateful for everything - thank you so much,

He hit Send.

Leaning back in his new desk chair, the Client smiled to himself. He looked out the office window and noticed it was starting to rain. Outside his second-floor office he could see a few shingles getting pelted with raindrops. He heard the sound of the coming storm, punched up with a single roll of thunder.

His life was not tidy. But nevertheless, he was smiling.

His wife's business was thriving. The bills were paid. Most importantly, his girls were doing really well in school. The lingering effects of the pandemic year were becoming less and less evident for his kids.

The Client was grateful.

Then his computer beeped. A new email.

He leaned forward in his chair to read it.

His largest client, the one that was buying a major new distributor, the one that had a big commission check for him, was apologizing.

They decided to back out of the purchase deal. Effective immediately. His services were no longer required. The contract was cancelled. He would be paid a pro-rated fee, through the end of the month. Which was three days from now.

That deal was his biggest source of revenue. In an instant, his wages were cut by two-thirds.

His oxygen was cut off.

His heart started racing. He was breathing through his nose, like a bull about to run. He cursed in a harsh whisper.

He wished he could retract the email he just sent to the Coach.

Just then, his wife tapped on the office door. She peeked inside. "Hi. How's it going?" she asked, stepping into his office.

He didn't turn around. He stared at the screen.

"Hey," she said, noticing he was frozen in place. "Is everything okay?"

He turned to her. "Well, I just got some really bad news."

He explained the situation. His biggest client had just pulled the plug. He had to find some new business. He hadn't planned on this happening. He wasn't sure what he was going to do. He pushed back his chair. Stood up. Turned to face his wife.

She hugged him. He felt the familiar embrace. His breathing settled down and he hugged her back. Held her, as she was holding him. Amidst his thoughts, which were racing, he slowed down. He found a speed where his situation was not his identity. His big client wasn't the only way to make money, he realized. He was still resourceful, still capable, still a guy with a game to play. And he was not alone.

"Oh! I'm so sorry," she said. "How do you feel?"

He looked at her. Kissed her. Pulled back and smiled at her. He felt her hands in the small of his back.

"This might sound strange, on a Tuesday morning," he said. "But I feel like it's a lazy Sunday afternoon."

RECOMMENDED READING

Livewired by David Eagleman (ISBN: 978-030-7907-493)
The Upside of Stress by Kelly McGonigal (ISBN: 978-110-1982-938)
Range by David Epstein (ISBN: 978-073-5214-507)
Deep Work by Cal Newport (ISBN: 978-034-9411-903)
Success from Anywhere by Karen Mangia (ISBN: 978-1-119-83462-5)
Company of One by Paul Jarvis (ISBN: 978-024-1380-222)

TED Talks

"Why Aren't We Awesomer?" by Michael Neill: https://bit.ly/easier-michaelneill
"Making Stress Your Friend," by Kelly McGonigal: https://bit.ly/easier-mcgonigal

Other Books by Chris Westfall

Leadership Language
The NEW Elevator Pitch
Bulletproof Branding

Social Media Links

Website: http://westfallonline.com
Facebook: /therealchriswestfall
Twitter: @westfallonline
Instagram: @westfallonline
LinkedIn: linkedin.com/in/westfallonline
YouTube: /westfallonline

ABOUT THE AUTHOR

Photo Credit: Magnolia Skye

Chris Westfall is a coach to executives, entrepreneurs, politicians, media personalities, and business leaders around the world. A regular contributor to *Forbes* on careers and leadership, his writing has appeared in *Entrepreneur, Success, U.S. News & World Report,* and many other publications. He is the author of *Leadership Language* (Wiley), *Bulletproof Branding,* and the international best-seller *The NEW Elevator Pitch.* He and his wife have two grown daughters and live in Texas.

ACKNOWLEDGMENTS

To those who have allowed me to be of service as a coach, I am honored by the trust you have placed in me. Serving you is a privilege. I am deeply grateful for the way you have allowed me to share this journey with you. Your progress continues to be a source of inspiration and hope for me.

To my very own Supercoach, Kristi Palma, thanks for showing me where the waves are. To my motivational experts, Sarah Kostin and Ken Orman, thanks for taking time to help me find the narrative when it wasn't always clear. And Russ Cusick – your HR expertise input was invaluable! Thank you for your talents and your friendship.

This project never would have come to life without the influence of my coaches and clients. To Michael Neill and Barb Patterson, I owe you a deep debt of gratitude. Your insights have shaped my own in powerful ways. Steve Chandler, what can I say? Call me.

To the team at Wiley, Jeanenne, Kezia, Dawn, Amy, and Chloé: Thank you for your understanding and your support. Kezia, we share a common thread, and your insights brought this story to a new level. The journey has been better because of you! To my promotional team, especially my assistant Gabriela Arraga, my sincere appreciation for helping me to know that I don't have to go it alone.

To my beautiful wife, Lisa-Gabrielle Greene: you are my lifeline and my support. Thank you for everything that you are. To my wonderful daughters, Ruby and Noli, you inspire me more than you know. I am so proud of both of you!

Finally, to you, the reader. Thank you for taking this journey. May you always find every possible way to make life easier. And help others to do the same.

INDEX